Socially
Responsible
Believers

Socially Responsible Believers

Puritans, Pietists, and Unionists in the History of the United Church of Christ

by Lowell H. Zuck

United Church Press
New York

Library of Congress Cataloging-in-Publication Data

Zuck, Lowell H.
   Socially responsible believers.

   Bibliography: p. 105.
   1. Reformed (Reformed Church)—Biography.
2. United Churches—clergy—Biography.   3. Puritans—
Biography.   4. Pietists—Biography.   5. Ecumenists—
Biography.   6. United Church of Christ—Biography.
I. Title.
BX9417.Z83   1986   284'.2'0922   [B]   86-25060
ISBN 0-8298-0744-6 (pbk.)

United Church Press, 132 West 31 Street, New York, New York 10001

Contents

Acknowledgments

During my first sabbatical leave from Eden Theological Seminary in 1964–65, I researched in Marburg, Germany, the democratic church order in the German Reformation, beginning with the 1526 Hessian Homberg synod. That fruitful learning experience deepened my commitment to examine European roots of the Evangelical and Reformed Church, since I had previously examined European Anabaptist contributions to the free-church tradition in my doctoral work with Roland H. Bainton. By 1975 that Anabaptist-Puritan study enabled me to publish a source book titled *Christianity and Revolution*.

In 1975–76 another Association of Theological Schools grant enabled me to visit additional libraries in the Netherlands, Switzerland, East and West Germany, and England. By that time I had broadened my institutional European and English reference points to origins of the United Church of Christ. Ironically, I wrote the Pilgrim Press booklet on European roots of the UCC while working in the London library of a Congregational college rich in Puritan sources. A bit on the side, I examined the liberal-confessional Reformed-Lutheran conflicts between Heinrich Heppe and August Vilmar in 1980, helped by the American Philosophical Society.

Throughout my work on European church history, I continued to study and teach American church history. By 1982 a National Endowment for the Humanities seminar in Baltimore enabled me to do research-publication work on Cotton Mather and Michael

Schlatter. I had previously published brief histories of the American UCC in general and in church growth contexts. Above all, it has been decades of the study and teaching of European and American church history at a rooted but ecumenical UCC seminary (Eden) that has allowed me to recover and transmit part of the rich heritage of a difficult and remarkable branch of the body of Christ. I am grateful to my family and to mentors, colleagues, administrators, and friends around the world who have helped to make possible this tribute to socially responsible believers who have helped to form a new American denomination growing from ancient roots.

Introduction

Finding common traits in a contemporary American denomination like the United Church of Christ is a difficult task, not to speak of describing coherent historical backgrounds for the most diffuse and transconfessional of all American churches. Nevertheless, that thirty-year-old church is gradually manifesting its own identity, and this book is a historical effort to depict its development centering on persons. The UCC might suitably be described throughout its various histories as a religious communion composed of socially responsible believers, based on Reformation and Puritan roots in Europe and England, and flowering amid the contributions made by American Puritans, Pietists, and Unionists. All the UCC traditions derive from personal belief based on Protestant confessions, mediated especially in a socially responsible tradition of a Reformed-free church type, here described as Puritan, Pietist, and/or Unionist. I shall refer to the three constituencies of the UCC as often overlapping Puritan, Pietist, and Unionist borderlines, but I maintain that wherever one or more of these emphases appeared, the characteristic UCC-type of socially responsible believing stance presented itself, among leaders and constituency alike, along with characteristic dissent, sometimes fearful and sometimes prophetic.

The study is made up of twenty-three historical case studies representative of UCC history rather than exhaustive or comprehensive of those rich and complex traditions. The intent of the case studies is to celebrate critically and appreciatively the stories of ordinary but memorable believers, whose commitments are embodied in living traditions of church, state, and culture in the USA and around the world. While I depict them within a milder pantheon than traditional martyr or hero or confession-oriented Christian history allows, our United Church socially responsible believers nevertheless represent authentic faith stances and healthy responsibility for the concerns of community going beyond the narrower limits of ecclesiastical history. A historical understanding of socially responsible believers should help a sometimes confused and disheartened church and community to discover its way again toward robust Christian confession in a perilous and many-sided world.

I look first at European roots of the UCC in Martin Luther's Protestant faith stance as mediated especially by his chief associate, the humanistic, educationally oriented, and conciliatory Philipp Melanchthon. The second form of Reformed faith is then described with special reference to the Swiss, French, and German Reformers—Ulrich Zwingli, John Calvin, and Zacharias Ursinus. I then make the chronological and geographical transition to England, where Puritan traditions, represented by John Browne, John Robinson, William Ames, and Oliver Cromwell, provided a major source for colonial American religious traditions. After the Reformation and Puritan roots in Europe and England have been treated, the remaining studies are centered on American Puritans, Pietists, and Unionists most typical of the various traditions making up the UCC after the mid-twentieth century. It is a long historical trip, but an exciting and relevant one.

I.
European
and
English
Roots

Chapter One
Reformation

1. Martin Luther— Philipp Melanchthon

No other individual in modern Western history affected so many people religiously as did an obscure German monk named Martin Luther. Yet understanding Luther is still problematic. As clear, definite, human, and religious as Luther evidently was, scholars and others still debate the precise meaning of his basic teaching— justification by faith—and his effects on church and state, whether medieval or modernizing, are still not altogether unquestioned. Nor is Luther's relation to the United Church of Christ very direct. We begin, necessarily, with the importance of the Protestant Reformation for our own backgrounds. Luther is overwhelmingly necessary to help explain the meaning of that same Reformation, its origin and purpose.

Luther's influence came to be especially related to people and churches of German and Scandinavian background, and those traditions are only partially represented within the UCC. For our Reformed and free churches, Luther's significance has been mediated through later Protestant traditions more than through Lutheran churches directly. We shall consider the work of Luther's chief educational disciple, Philipp Melanchthon, as having special significance for our churches, after we look briefly at Luther's teachings and activities.

The general outlines of Luther's life are well known. He was born more than 500 years ago, in 1483, as a miner's son of upwardly mobile peasant German stock. At age twenty-two Luther gave up his obedient professional advancement toward the legal profession to become an Augustinian monk in Erfurt, seeking his soul's salvation after narrowly escaping a threatening thunderbolt on a summer day.

Luther's consequent spiritual doubts, "seeking a just and merciful God," came to be resolved for him through biblical exegesis in the course of his normal teaching responsibilities. Like Augustine of Hippo a millennium earlier, Luther reclaimed with joy the biblical teaching of justification by faith through God's grace, affirming that God through the gift of Christ comes to stand at a person's side, making the believer a partaker of Christ's righteousness and all Christ's qualities.[1]

That newfound faith helped the humble monk to become an unwitting reformer, as the unreformed church of his day attempted unsuccessfully to silence Luther's questions about the faithfulness of its indulgence salesmanship. Luther's subsequent career underwent the usual disappointments and betrayals, and ambiguities troubled his seemingly forthright positions. Although Luther's theology desacralized material objects and abolished sacred pretensions of church and secular authority, he appeared to have restored the divine authority of princes, when in 1525 he criticized radical peasant demands, having previously introduced a "two-realms" teaching. Nevertheless, the constructive element of Luther's ethics that "faith works by love" moved his influence beyond individual piety into an effective social gospel for the modern world. Luther thus had an impact on all parts of the present UCC, rather than merely evoking a pious memory from those who were formerly German Evangelicals![2]

The most helpful younger colleague to Luther at the new, biblically oriented Wittenberg theological faculty was Philipp Melanchthon (1497–1560), a linguistic genius whose great uncle was the humanist and pioneer Hebrew scholar Johannes Reuchlin. Beginning as professor of Greek at Wittenberg in 1518, the twenty-one-year-old Erasmian humanist scholar quickly turned to the ancient source of salvation, the Bible, under Luther's powerful influence. By 1521 Melanchthon had written the first systematic theology of the Reformation, the *Loci Communes* (Common Places). Luther praised Melanchthon's work extravagantly as the best book next to the Bible. Melanchthon never fulfilled Luther's wish for him to be ordained as a Protestant minister. But their friendship never failed. At the same time, Melanchthon's continuing humanist commitments gave his theology a slightly different slant from that of Luther's. He naturally emphasized more than Luther the role of reason and free will in humanity, as well as being willing to explain the real presence of Christ in the Lord's Supper more dynamically and less metaphysically than Luther.

In practical matters of reform, no one served Luther and the Reformation more effectively than Melanchthon. The basic Protestant confession of faith, the 1530 and 1540 Augsburg Confession, was written by Melanchthon because Luther, as a condemned heretic, could not attend a diet of the empire. The official visitations of parishes and schools after 1525, which actually brought the Reformation into existence, were conducted according to criteria drawn up by Melanchthon. He introduced new teaching methods everywhere the Reformation penetrated and drew up new constitutions organizing Lutheran churches. Melanchthon, from that day to this, has been described as the "Praeceptor of Germany." He should also be called the "Teacher or Doctor of the Church."[3] No one else comes close to the educational effect that Melanchthon had on establishing Latin schools and universities in Germany—a positive contribution indeed.

On the more controversial side, Melanchthon became a threatened leader of one of the two Lutheran parties after Luther's death in 1546. Political and dogmatic differences contributed to the inner-Lutheran disputes. Hesse and Electoral Saxony were rivals at the beginning of the Reformation. Ducal Saxony then came into conflict with Electoral Saxony. Later, Electoral Saxony disapproved of Palatinate theology and politics, involving differences also between Lutheran and Reformed churches in the two regions, as we shall see. Melanchthon did what he could to uphold his distinctive views, accused by stricter Lutherans of heretical synergistic, works righteousness, and symbolic Lord's Supper views, and was thus put on the defensive.

To some extent, Melanchthon's position and party carried on the *unitive* side of the Reformation, which could also be found in some of Luther's attitudes. From its beginnings the Reformation has manifested *unitive* as well as *dissenting* tendencies.[4] Melanchthon, more than Luther, sought re-union with the Catholic Church and, less clearly, with other Protestants. Luther did not regard his own movement as a dissenting sect,[5] but rather as the true church. He saw evangelicals as cleansing the whole catholic church of false doctrine and misconduct. Insofar as Luther approved or tolerated Melanchthon's revision of the Catholic unitive Augsburg Confession (1530) in the direction of Reformed convictions (1540), Luther abetted the unitive thrust of the Reformation.

2.
Ulrich
Zwingli

Lutheran Reformers called on pious territorial princes for aid. They had less success enlisting support from independent city councils. It was in Switzerland and the Rhineland, in Zurich, Strassburg, and Geneva, that the Reformed faith appealed to independent city councils. Although Ulrich Zwingli (1484–1531) had a key role in introducing the Swiss Reformation, the "lords of the council" in Zurich and other cities had been accustomed to regulating affairs since the Middle Ages and were more confident than the small-town politicians of the Saxon cities, where Lutheranism predominated.[6]

Wittenberg and Zurich were different cities, not only politically, but also socially, representative of Germany and Switzerland, respectively. Zurich was a sovereign, aristocratic-democratic city-state. Its religious politics were largely independent, weakly related as the church was to the Catholic bishop of Constance. As religious leader in Zurich, Zwingli had to be active in social politics as well as in church politics. Persuading the city council was basic to introducing Swiss Reformation in 1523. On the contrary, Luther worked in a prince-dominated patriarchal feudal state, where political and social activities were more circumscribed. Luther had his own way of keeping in touch with politics, but it is no accident that Lutheranism developed a carefully prescribed "two-kingdoms" doctrine.

Ulrich Zwingli[7] was born less than three months after Luther, into a German-speaking family whose background was similar to that of Luther's family. His father was a village magistrate. An uncle, who was a priest, lived nearby and began teaching the bright young man. After Latin school in Basel and Bern, Zwingli attended the universities of Vienna and Basel. Being educated as a humanist much more than was Luther, he was ordained as a priest in 1506. Also unlike Luther, he had little theological education and no monastic experience.

Zwingli served for a decade as priest in Glarus, where he wrote against the evils of Swiss mercenary service in foreign armies. A fine humanistic scholar, Zwingli, following Erasmus, studied the original texts of the Church Fathers and the Greek New Testament in his spare time. From 1516 to 1518 Zwingli attacked the veneration of relics and indulgences while he was pastor at the famous pilgrimage shrine of the Black Virgin at Einsiedeln. A biblical scholar but not yet a Protestant in theology, he was called to be people's priest at the cathedral church of Zurich, the Grossmünster. His appointment found approval despite his openly confessed guilt in sexual lapses, common among Swiss clergy of that era.

Zwingli became a bold, prophetic pastor in Zurich, where he introduced changes in the church with great effectiveness after 1519. He preached in the Grossmünster with a verse-by-verse exegesis of Matthew. He introduced "prophesying,"[8] a separate meeting for mutual exposition of sermons and discussion that was much admired and used by Elizabethan Puritans. Zwingli sought to erect a Christian community, a prophetic commonwealth, a city under the Word. Before Calvin, Zwingli, depending on Zurich civic reform, pioneered in erecting a disciplined church and commonwealth molded by an active, earnest faith. Repudiating the notion that sensible things convey spiritual grace, Zwingli also introduced Puritan simplicity and Reformed austerity in forms of worship.

More specifically, Zwingli's program after 1516 was still Erasmian, based on recovering gospel teachings from the Greek New Testament. It is probable that Zwingli's disappointment over Luther's excommunication in 1520 broke through Zwingli's humanistic optimism. At any rate, Zwingli became fully evangelical in the same sense as Luther and under Luther's influence early in 1521.[9] During Lent in 1522 Zwingli openly supported Froschauer, a printer, when he disobeyed the fasting laws, and Zwingli's first Reformation writing appeared, "About Choosing and Liberty of Food." Early in 1523 the city council approved Zwingli's "Sixty-seven Theses" at the First Zurich Disputation, issuing a demand that all ministers henceforth preach the new evangelical doctrines.

Zurich moved fairly quickly toward further reformation. But Catholic opposition and more radical, congregational, separatist tendencies complicated the task for Zwingli and the city council. Radical destruction of images forced the calling of a Second Zurich Disputation in October 1523, concerning images and the mass. A moderate decision followed, encouraging orderly removal of images. The first instance of Anabaptist tendencies in Switzerland emerged in radical opposition to the council's decision. The opposition was led by pioneer Swiss-German Anabaptists Conrad Grebel and Balthasar Hübmaier. Elements emerging among these opponents of Zwingli were defined more moderately by later English Congregationalists. The direct descendants of the Swiss dissidents are the modern Mennonites.[10]

By 1525, when Zwingli published his "Commentary on True and False Religion," the Zurich Reformation had broken sharply with Catholic teachings and practice. Not only had the mass been abolished, but also organs, choirs, altars, processions, relics, and images. A new marriage law was proclaimed, and new ways of caring for the poor and for reforming schools were introduced.

Compared with Luther, Zwingli was more an ethical than a dogmatic theologian of Reformation. Like Melanchthon, he was a radical humanist. Unlike Calvin, he worked as a radical politician. The most modern of the Reformers, he can be seen as a predecessor of liberal theology, a path-breaker for undogmatic, free Christianity. Secular historians see Zwingli as the founder of evangelical state-church Christianity, noting how he introduced the Reformation as a political power. On some points Zwingli was more traditional than Luther, for example, in Mariology, and he remained firm on upholding the tradition requiring infant baptism. His Lord's Supper teaching was not so radical as some later critics have thought, and his *respublica christiana* idea was traditional and theological in origin, not humanistic or legalistic.

Zwingli was a social theologian, wishing the *regnum Christi* to be *in,* not *above,* the world, spreading in society, city, and state, not only among single confessors and Christian families.[11] His salvation teaching urged not only otherwordly salvation, but also innerworldly healing of the community-church, aiding the historical appearance of the people of God in a moral, living community. This all sprang up amid the bourgeois republic of Zurich, in a federal, aristocratic society.

The world into which Zwingli came was unsure and restless. The Swiss were caught between the power of the Hapsburg kaiser, the French king, and the Roman pope. Zwingli fought first as a Swiss patriot against France's control of northern Italy. Later, as a political, churchly Reformer, he contested the worldly power of the Roman Church in Switzerland. Finally, as a leading Zurich citizen, Zwingli sought, in covenant with France, to halt Austrian ambitions in eastern Switzerland. In all these activities, Zwingli urged adoption of a *social* idea of freedom, the *political* freedom of the Christian congregation, the *moral* freedom of bourgeois common life, and *spiritual* freedom for open preaching. Zwingli's goal was not abstract individual freedom, but concrete, bourgeois freedom. His motto was: "Don't suffer, fight!" His symbol was the sword, not the cross. His activity was also humanist-oriented, seeking spiritual community, also with the Fathers of the ancient Church. To Zwingli, the Church Fathers were more important than contemporary theologians.

Unlike Luther's doctrine of the two kingdoms. Zwingli's kingdom of Chirst is not eschatologically distant, but present within the elect community of God. The visible church appears, according to Zwingli, also in the politically organized local church; legally, it is fully independent: "the *ecclesia visibilis,* the word 'church,' is used for the separate gathering, with its preachers and hearers."[12] Each congregation is also responsible for its outer regulation. Not only his Anabaptist opponents, but Zwingli himself helped to develop congregational theory.

At the same time Zwingli emphasized the unity of political and religious community, a real theocracy. He never tried to set up a system in which God's representative directed the policies of government, which is what moderns mean by theocracy. He pursued a wider theocratic goal, seeking to free the clergy from concerns of worldly wealth and power so that they might preach the gospel and not interfere with the magistrate's performance of the duties God had assigned him. Zwingli assumed that only where the clergy and the secular ruler fulfilled the obligations that they had to a Christian society could the will of God be realized, and he knew no other purpose for the community than to follow the divine will.

In practice, Zwingli's practically oriented theology failed, amid the complications of Swiss religious-political divisions. His career was cut short by his death in 1531, at age forty-seven. He died while serving as chaplain for the Reformed troops on the battlefield at Cappel, against a host of Catholic Swiss forces outnumbering the Zurichers.

3.
John
Calvin

In Germany the Evangelical Church developed slowly, since Luther's reform, directed against Roman Catholic doctrinal teachings, allowed more room for questions of faith than for practical matters of church organization and discipline (the latter concerns were more typical of later Reformed and Congregational church people). A union effort in 1529 at Marburg, Germany, brought Luther, Martin Bucer, and Zwingli into agreement on fifteen articles of faith, but disagreement about the real presence of Christ in the Lord's Supper in the last article caused the Lutherans and Zwinglians to depart unreconciled doctrinally.

Martin Bucer (1491–1551) in Strassburg, Calvin's mentor, through his whole career until his death as an exiled professor in England, actively sought to make peace between disagreeing theologians and quarreling churches.[13] The influence of Bucer greatly increased through the work of John Calvin (1509–64),[14] closer to Luther's theology than to Zwingli's, who rapidly became the most significant Reformer after Luther. When Calvin, a second-generation Reformer, arrived on the scene in 1536, the early Reformed Church was already passing into the second of its three stages, from German-Swiss, through French-Swiss, and then into further expansion around 1563 as a German Reformed movement. The successive centers of Reformed faith were Zurich, Geneva, and Heidelberg.

As the Lutheran Reformation spread through northern Germany and into Scandinavia, certain sections of Germany become receptive to a form of Lutheranism having affinities to the Reformed faith. Hesse, the powerful state of the Landgrave Philipp, had earlier provided the site for the abortive ecumenical peace conference between Luther and Zwingli at Philipp's castle in Marburg. Prince Philipp, called the Magnanimous, had early allied himself with the new Protestant faith, established the first Protestant university in 1527 at Marburg, and actively pursued his conviction that evangelical unity was an overriding political necessity.

Because of his accomplishments in reforming Strassburg, Martin Bucer was called on to organize Protestant churches in other cities as well, including Ulm, Augsburg, and Constance, and in the territory of Hesse. Philipp worked closely with Bucer, hoping to unite the German and Swiss movements of reformation, for political as well as for religious purposes. At the Marburg Colloquy, however, Luther had declared that Bucer, like Zwingli, was of another spirit from his own. When division between Catholics and evangelicals deepened in the late 1520s, Melanchthon's moderate Augsburg Confession failed to overcome eucharistic division with the Swiss. Bucer then set forth the Tetrapolitan Confession of the South German Reformers (near to the Swiss) over against the Augsburg Confession.[15] Forced to flee to England from Strassburg, Bucer contributed to emerging Anglican liturgical reform in a less rigid manner than did the Lutherans and more in accord with the later spirit of the united churches.

Zurich was fortunate in finding a wise and moderate successor to Zwingli in Henry Bullinger (1504–75).[16] An exemplary pastor and teacher, carrying on a vast correspondence all over Europe, Bullinger fits well into our United Church story because he became the favorite continental Reformer for exiled English Protestants, thus not only contributing to the views of emerging English Presbyterians and Congregationalists, but also having significant impact on Anglican faith and liturgical forms. By 1566 Bullinger's "Second Helvetic Confession" was commending itself widely beyond Switzerland as a standard Reformed doctrinal norm. His sermons, widely reprinted and required reading for English clergy, marked a transition beyond Zwingli's views into the greater churchly and theological achievements of John Calvin.

The son of a notary in episcopal service, the Frenchman John Calvin was precocious in legal, humanistic, and theological studies. Educated with a noble son of a family associated with the local Catholic cathedral in Noyon, Calvin studied liberal arts in Paris. Completing the study of law in Orleans and Bourges, Calvin also became increasingly interested in humanism, especially as represented by the older scholar and Christian humanist Faber Stapulensis. Turning, after the death of his father, to a possible career as learned humanist commentator on classic writings, Calvin did publish a commentary on the pagan philosopher Seneca's work *De clementia*.

Suddenly, around age twenty-three, Calvin made the irrevocable conversion move from humanistic scholarship to evangelical faith, and within a year he was forced to flee France as a notorious heretic. He was always reticent about personal matters, so the precise process or reason for his conversion remains unclear. His progress in attaining personal clarity of faith and ability to communicate it were amazing.

As a refugee in Basel, Calvin published a small catechism, the *Institutes of the Christian Religion,* in 1536. This immediately established him as a leading interpreter of Protestant thought and life. Later editions, in 1539 and especially 1559, gave the *Institutes* worldwide influence in training ministers and establishing Reformed churches. Detouring through Geneva on his way toward work as a scholar in Basel, Calvin was prevailed on by a choleric fellow French Reformer, Wilhelm Farel, to help reform the unruly city of Geneva. There, with a fruitful interlude of exile in Strassburg from 1538 to 1541, Calvin spent the remainder of his life in a ministry that one of his most influential followers, the Scotsman John Knox, called "the most perfect school of Christ and the apostles."

Beginning as a modest teacher of scripture in the church of Geneva, Calvin developed further the emphases of the Basel Reformer Oecolampadius and of Bucer that the church must control its pastoral discipline. Unsuccessful in their first attempt at pastoral control against the interference of the council, Calvin and Farel were banished from Geneva. As pastor of a French refugee congregation in Strassburg, Calvin grew notably from 1538 to 1541. Bucer influenced him in developing his own way of combining pastoral care with discipline, making use of the biblical model of pastors, teachers, elders, and deacons.[17] Calvin's simpler liturgy was based on the liturgy of Strassburg.

When Calvin was invited back to Geneva in 1541, he was able to institute his presbyterian system of church government, appointing pastors, teachers, elders, and deacons. The town council still refused the church elders the right to impose sanctions or excommunicate independently, a right not won for the church by Calvin until 1555. In the meantime, Calvin was developing his full church-state doctrine that clearly distinguished between civil and ecclesiastical discipline, while Zurich moved in a more Erastian direction, with its doctrine of the godly magistrate tending toward domination over the church.

Calvin's *Institutes,* appearing in a final edition in 1559, made the Reformed tradition consistent and palatable with a formidable doctrine of the sovereign grace of God. Displaying great knowledge of scripture and a majestic sense of divine providence, Calvin knit the doctrines of Word and Spirit into a harmonious whole. For him, the Word again went forth to conquer, as Luther's early vision had prophesied. Insisting on a true spiritual presence of Christ in the Lord's Supper, Calvin was able to heal some festering doctrinal wounds among Protestants. More than any other person save Luther, Calvin manifested the power and exhilaration of Protestant faith and theology at their best, submissive to God's grace and sovereignty and obedient to the Lord Jesus Christ.

No Reformer besides Luther has had the worldwide influence that Calvin has had on a whole family of Reformed-Presbyterian churches speaking many languages expanded over the whole world. His influence is far wider than is represented in the parts of the UCC affected most by Reformed-Congregational theology and practice. Yet no American churches come closer to original Calvinistic roots in Switzerland than present-day UCC churches, many of whom have become unaware of their historic rootage in a major branch of the Protestant movement.

4.
Zacharias
Ursinus

In this final section on the Reformation, I make the transition by way of Zwingli, Calvin, and their successors beyond the Swiss Reformed Church, with its German- and French-speaking centers, to the German Reformed Church centered at Heidelberg after the 1560s. The expansion of Reformed churches into Germany depends, to some extent, on the revival of Zwinglianism by Henry Bullinger, his Swiss successor. Rebuffed by Luther and Bucer, Bullinger was able to reach an accord with Calvin in the 1549 Zurich "Consensus,"[18] and by 1567 the "Second Helvetic Confession" of Bullinger had given doctrinal status to Zwinglianism after all and manifested the unity of expanding Swiss Reformed faith. Zwingli had failed to mediate his faith to Germany through Philipp of Hesse. Now Bullinger's Zwinglian-Calvinism found a territorial home in the Palatinate near Heidelberg with the assistance of the Elector Palatine Frederick III, called the "Pious."

At the same time, the peculiar character of the German Reformed Church made it a mediator between Wittenberg, Zurich, and Geneva, and its theological origins lay also in Melanchthon's Wittenberg as well as in Calvin's Geneva. As one would expect in the German lands, the Swiss model of Reformation carried out by autonomous city-states was subordinated to the reforming interests of territorial princes, whether mighty or humble. In the case of the Elector Palatine Frederick III, we owe the introduction of the Reformed faith into Germany to the personal religious-political actions of that most powerful statesman in Germany next to the emperor. Elector Otto Heinrich introduced the Reformation into the Palatinate in 1556, having had drawn up a church order combining simple South German Württemberg Lutheran forms with other observances from Zurich, Strassburg, and Geneva. Otto Heinrich was childless, and his line was followed in 1559 by Frederick III from Pfalz-Simmern.[19] Frederick was educated in a pious Catholic court at Nancy and Brussels, but his marriage to Mary of Brandenburg-Kulmbach, a Lutheran, moved him to become a Protestant. Confessional differences over the Lord's Supper flared up, and Frederick was forced to mediate at Heidelberg between the strict Lutheran superintendent Hesshus and a Reformed deacon named Klebitz.

The Lutheran view of the presence of Christ in the Supper was that if all that is offered is a spiritual Christ, it is of no value to the Christian, threatened by the death of the body. The Supper has to do only with the concrete, historical Christ, our Savior. The Reformed said, on the contrary, that because they put so much stress on the incarnate, historical Christ, they taught that he was now *ascended,* and hence not physically present in the Supper, as he will be again after his return. They thought that they were clearer and more biblical than the Lutherans.

In the end, Frederick discharged both opponents, finding useful a compromise formula drawn up by Melanchthon. At a gathering of princes at Naumburg in 1561, Frederick came into conflict with his colleagues because he insisted on using the revised form (1540) of the Augsburg Confession, regarding the Lord's Supper. He then moved rapidly toward introducing the Reformed faith into the Palatinate, removing pictures, altars, baptismal fonts, and organs from the churches and appointing two young theologians to draw up a new creed and order of worship. These two able collaborators in writing the Heidelberg Catechism were Caspar Olevianus and Zacharias Ursinus.[20] The two founders of the German Reformed Church, although differing in having Calvinist over against Melanchthonian training, and contrastingly pastoral and professorial in manner, had remarkably parallel careers nevertheless.

Born at Trier in the west, Olevianus (1536–87) studied law at Paris, Orleans, and Bourges, like Calvin. He sympathized with the sufferings of the French Protestants, which affected him deeply. Through the study of theology in Geneva, Olevianus came to know Calvin well. Born at Breslau (Silesia) in the east, Ursinus (1534–83) was taught Protestant theology in his home city by Ambrosius Moibanus and then studied at Wittenberg under Melanchthon.[21] Seven years later he continued his theological education at

Heidelberg, Strassburg, and Basel and was then welcomed to Geneva by Calvin. Ursinus completed his wandering, educational tour of Europe by visiting Lyon, Orleans, and Paris. Both young theologians ended their student years at Zurich, thereby demonstrating Reformed tendencies, whatever their Lutheran backgrounds might have been. They were together with Henry Bullinger when the successor of Zwingli was drafting a student catechism in 1558 and 1559.

Olevianus returned to his native city, Trier, as a preacher of the Reformation. Successful, he later had to escape with his life when the local Catholic archbishop reacted violently. He then became a teacher at Heidelberg (1560) and was soon appointed to a university chair of dogmatics. In 1562 he became court preacher and church counselor in Heidelberg. Ursinus returned to his native Breslau as a teacher but had to leave when he was accused of denying the real presence of Christ in the Lord's Supper in his "Theses de Sacramentis" (1559). Fleeing to Zurich, where Bullinger and Peter Martyr Vermigli supported him, Ursinus in 1561 joined Olevianus as one of the newly installed professors at Heidelberg University, in process of adopting the Reformed faith.

Ursinus took over the dogmatics teaching at Heidelberg when Olevianus resumed preaching and came to exercise additional church leadership. Prince Frederick then appointed Ursinus leader of the Sapience College, where he greatly influenced theological developments. Ursinus, along with others, was able to reshape the theological character of the Palatinate, entering into the triumph of Melanchthonian and Reformed doctrine at Heidelberg over strong Lutheran tendencies up to the Thirty Years' War.

At Heidelberg the earlier church order of Otto Henry had depended on the scriptures and the Augsburg Confession and included Melanchthon's examination for ordination of pastors and the children's catechism of Johannes Brenz.[22] In the schools, Luther's *Small Catechism* had been used, along with others, including one from Regensburg.[23] Frederick III now asked Ursinus to prepare two new theological works, a "Summa" of teaching in Latin and a short catechism in German. They comprised 323 and 108 questions and answers, respectively. The "Summa" was to be for students and elders (i.e., Latin scholars); the catechism was aimed at educating children and common people. In the newly drawn up church order it served in both ways: as means of examination for ordination and as a source of catechetical training of children (no mean task to accomplish together!). Ursinus' manuscript was partly in Latin, according to the custom of the time. His colleague Peter Boquin held that the German form was not altogether valid. The "Summa" for theologians was a masterful effort combining Calvin's views with a modified covenant theology of Bullinger and with the theological definitions of the law-gospel, nature-grace dichotomies of Melanchthon.

Few Reformation documents have so harmonized different theological conceptions as the Heidelberg Catechism. It is a complete dogmatic compendium. In contrast with later catechisms, it does not treat controversial questions. The form is not only clearer than others, but also more catechetical and more concrete, even in its abstract theological definitions, where an answering "I" is demanded. Most of the federal-theological underpinning disappears; covenant theology appears only as an auxiliary teaching to justify the baptism of infants. Its basic division is into three parts, recognizing human participation in the misery of sin, divine provision of the means of salvation, and, again, human thanksgiving.

It has often been said that the Heidelberg Catechism was not original. Melanchthon's catechism had been used in the Palatinate, as were the Zurich and Geneva catechisms, especially the latter, which Ursinus translated into German. The Augsburg Confession, the Emden Catechism, Beza's Confession, and the Strassburg Catechism, along with other theological works by Calvin, Bullinger, Melanchthon, and Thomas Erastus, were used in preparing the Heidelberg Catechism. A commission including Prince Frederick did the final editing of the catechism and church order, but contemporary scholars maintain that Ursinus did most of the work.[24]

Visser summarized in the following way Ursinus' remarkable ability to thread his way between competing theological positions in the Heidelberg Catechism:

> Ursinus cannot be categorized as belonging to any school or movement other than the evangelical church. Like Calvin, he stood with Luther in affirming justification by faith alone. He did not follow Melanchthon in the latter's synergism, for he believed man by himself could do nothing. Good works were a thanksgiving and a duty consequent upon justification. On the issue of predestination he also stood close to both Calvin and Luther and in his *Admonition* he chastised the Lutherans for deviating from Luther's position. . . . He modified the doctrine of double predestination by accepting the doctrine of permission. On the

meaning of the sacraments he can be placed with Calvin, but as he himself continued to argue, also with Melanchthon and in some aspects even with Luther. On the presence of Christ in the Lord's Supper, he thought like Calvin and Melanchthon, but he went so far as to accept Lutheran phraseology as long as he was allowed to give it a Reformed interpretation and as long as it excluded the doctrine of the ubiquity of Christ's human body.[25]

As a person, Ursinus appears to have been melancholy, even suicidal. He was retiring and disliked camaraderie. Yet he worked exceedingly hard and effectively. A true Melanchthonian, he turned from the ancient classics to a Reformation quest for God and human salvation. Instead of Luther's question, "How can I find a gracious God?" or Calvin's conviction in his catechism that "the principal end of human life is to know God so as to render Him the honor due Him," Ursinus asked and found answers to a Melanchthonian question: "What is my only trust in life and in death?"

More dynamic and experiential than Calvin's definition of faith as "firm and sure knowledge of the love of God for us," Ursinus asserted that "it is not only by sure knowledge that I hold for true what God has revealed to us in His Word, it is also by a trusting heart which the Holy Spirit produces in me through the Gospel." On the Lord's Supper, Calvin taught that "as Jesus Christ promises us and represents to us in the symbols of bread and wine, I do not doubt he makes us participants of His own substance so that we may live from His own life." More dynamic again, Ursinus asserted that consuming the holy elements "means not only accepting with a believing heart all the passion and death of Christ, but also being more and more united to the sacred body of Christ, through the Holy Spirit who dwells in Him and in us, so much so that though he is in heaven and we are on earth we are nevertheless flesh of his flesh and bone of his bone." It also represented a more idealistic, less mysterious view of how believers are sacramentally united with Christ.

Religiously, Ursinus accomplished a double task: to restate clearly the common Reformation basis of the five main points of Luther's *Small Catechism* of 1529 (law, faith, prayer, baptism, and the Lord's Supper) as well as to make a distinctly Reformed faith statement. The note of living and dying unto Christ came not only out of Ursinus' pained attitude toward life, but also from a severe, eighteen-month plague that afflicted Heidelberg. His *Christian* perspective was inseparably connected with humanity, and contrasted to Calvin, the Heidelberg Catechism was anthropocentric rather than theocentric, emphasizing *my* salvation rather than the honor of God.[26] Ursinus was fully one with Luther in emphasizing the good news of God's justification of the sinner through faith, treating the five points of the catechism with equal or greater severity and bringing out even more than Luther the note of obedience and joy: "Where there is forgiveness of sins, life and blessedness result [*Small Catechism*]."

Theologically, Ursinus differed significantly from both Luther and his own mentor, Melanchthon. On the Lord's Supper and the person of Christ he advocated a Reformed view, which entangled him in polemical encounters with strict Lutherans for the remainder of his life. The Lord's Supper, Ursinus taught, is *not* reception of the bodily presence of Christ, but a visible sign and seal (as is baptism) that the risen Christ brings forgiveness of sins and eternal life to his own people. On the person of Christ, instead of Lutheran communication of the two natures, Ursinus taught that Christ's human nature is presently "at the right hand of his Father in heaven"; the divine nature of Christ remains present with us. For this reason Christ is spiritually present with us, but his physical presence will only be restored when he comes again in the last days. Theologically, Ursinus, in this sense, anticipated Protestant orthodoxy, teaching that doctrine is systematic and willing to fight for the truth, over his personal inclinations.

Ursinus was removed from his Heidelberg position in 1578 because the new Elector, Ludwig, after the death of Frederick in 1576, was a Lutheran, purging his realm of Calvinists. Frederick's younger son, Johann Casimir, loyal to the Reformed faith of his father, then established a new Reformed university, the Casimirianum, at Neustadt on the Haardt, with Ursinus as its leading theologian. Olevianus had moved to Herborn, where another significant Reformed school began. At Neustadt, Ursinus lectured on the prophet Isaiah and published the *Admonition,* his most comprehensive rebuttal to the Lutheran *Book of Concord,* loyal as he was to the spirit and theology of Melanchthon. Unable to realize his dream of a Europe-wide evangelical synod, Ursinus died at Neustadt in 1583, only forty-three years old, in the same year the Reformed faith returned to Heidelberg.

Melanchton's best and most gifted pupil, Ursinus was a true mediating theologian, blending Melanchthonian and Calvinist theology in a fresh way, while also making use of Aristotelian philosophical methods. Ursinus gave an alternative direction to non-Lutheran theology in Germany. The Heidelberg Catechism, his chief monument, became one of the most widespread religious publications in world literature, and it has been translated into a host of languages—more than two hundred versions in all.[27]

Chapter Two
Puritan

In addition to its basic continental and English Reformation roots, the UCC goes back to a predominant English origin derived from Puritanism, together with an allied continental tradition of Pietism. In this chapter I shall look briefly at the English Puritan tradition so far as it pertains to the UCC. The terms Puritan and Pietist have powerful meaning but are used in such contradictory ways that it is necessary to set forth some definitions.

"Puritan" pertains especially to English developments, and "Pietist" centers predominantly in a German Lutheran movement begun with P.J. Spener's pious conventicles around 1670. Some historians going back to Heinrich Heppe have argued that Pietism had its origin among earlier English Puritans, and August Lang regarded the German Bucer as the first Puritan and William Perkins, an Englishman, as the first Pietist![28] This effort to connect seemingly different movements resembles our description of the eventual union of UCC constituents, English, German, and others, as including some common theological and communal roots in history. At any rate, Puritans and Pietists were not without mutual relations from the beginning.

A subgroup of English Puritanism, Separatism, and eventual nonconformity, the "Congregational Way" (a major component of the UCC) emerged as a distinctive and powerful expression of English church life.[29] Obscure in specific origins because of its appearance among popular Separatism during the reign of Queen Elizabeth, Congregationalism developed into militant religious Independency during the Interregnum dominated by victorious Lord Protector Oliver Cromwell.[30]

After King Henry VIII had broken with the Church of Rome, making himself Supreme Head of the Church of England in 1534, an established Protestant church separate from Rome became the basic condition of English ecclesiastical history.[31] English Catholics became a party out of touch with the most influential forces in the nation. The official church had little to fear from Catholics in England.

It was otherwise with Protestantism, precisely because of the theologically comprehensive type of non-Romanism that the great Tudor monarchs preferred. The labels Puritans, Separatists, and nonconformists refer in different ways to Protestants in England who wished further reformation of the Church of England, as do the later denominational labels Presbyterians, Independents or Congregationalists, Baptists, and Quakers.

After the culmination of Protestant dissatisfaction with the church and nation in revolution around 1640, the denominational names became predominant. When the Anglican establishment was restored in 1660, marking the failure of more extreme Protestants to secure establishment, the denominations were becoming known, at least by their enemies, as "dissenters" or "nonconformists" or, later and more positively, as the "English free churches."[32]

When they first appeared on the English scene in Elizabethan days, the radical Protestants were nicknamed "Puritans," and that imprecise but widely used label has persisted, along with much inaccuracy as to just what Puritanism entailed. Today, Puritans are seen by many as moralizing believers, out of touch with the realities of life and the world. When they first appeared, in the midst of an officially Christian society, Puritans were the most dynamic element of society, representing permanently valid attitudes toward culture and faith.

Most precisely, Puritans were dissenters (not necessarily Separatists) from official Elizabethan Anglican liturgies, ceremonies, and discipline (or lack of it) in all sorts of churches, including a strong representation within the Church of England. They developed new dynamic personalities, making use of rationality based on literacy along with a kind of narrow biblical literalism, and they appealed to the new middle class of England that combined a passion for trade and a hatred for monopolies with a passion for personal religious encounter with God involving the development of conscience and rigid honesty. Not so much a creed or party in the beginning, Puritans developed an attitude of mind clinging to the letter of scripture, seeking spiritual worship, and manifesting a Calvinistic or Reformed disposition to regard as idolatrous all that we have superimposed on the Word of God.[33] Intensity, simplicity, and universal sainthood within the church characterized Puritanism, the latter in a secular form resulting in democracy.

This Puritanism may be described as peculiarly English, involving a uniquely English response to both the Renaissance and the Reformation. At the same time it mediated the more radical forms of continental Protestantism to England, especially the Reformed faith, and, less clearly, the Anabaptist faith. Persons and writings brought in continental influences. Exiles coming to England, such as the German Bucer and the Italian Peter Martyr Vermigli, introduced the Reformed faith and liturgical style to Cambridge and Oxford during the reign of Edward VI, as did the Pole Jan Laski at London and the Frenchman Valérand Poullain at Glastonbury, in their refugee congregations.[34]

Equally important were the English Puritan exiles leaving England during the Catholic restoration of Queen Mary Tudor. They absorbed Reformed ideas in Switzerland and Germany, returning as a kind of radical party of hope when Queen Elizabeth was enthroned in 1558. Bishop John Hooper of Gloucester, exiled earlier during Henry VIII's reign, becoming a radical Zwinglian abroad, returned to inaugurate opposition to wearing vestments as a matter of Puritan conscience.[35] Lang thought that Hooper, influenced by Bullinger, should be described as "the second Puritan-Pietist," after Martin Bucer. Hooper was burned at the stake for heresy by Queen Mary in 1555. The frequent burnings of Protestants under Mary served only to make the Puritan movement better known.

While the exiles were abroad, the more radical of them urged separation from an unreformed Church of England. In Frankfurt, Germany, followers of the Scotsman John Knox (1505–72) separated from the Coxians, who continued to use the Book of Common Prayer in worship, while the Knoxians insisted on adaptation of Calvin's freer Geneva order of worship. Back in Scotland, Knox and his Presbyterian associates became the most powerful element of the Puritan movement. In the meantime the first underground Separatists appeared in London in 1567. Richard Fitz and his "Plumbers Hall" group were seized and imprisoned. Slightly earlier at Cambridge, presbyterian principles were advocated by the professor of divinity, Thomas Cartwright (1535–1603), who was also removed from his position. Others carried on Cartwright's presbyterian experiments and congregational prophesyings.

1.
Robert
Browne

Cartwright, amid all his troubles, opposed separation. The first conspicuous advocate of Separatism in England was Robert Browne (c. 1550-1633), a graduate of Cambridge.[36] Browne was born in Tolethorpe (Rutland), England, into a well-established family. The great Elizabethan statesman William Cecil (later Lord Burghley) was his near relative. In 1570 Browne became a student in Corpus Christi College, Cambridge, at a time when controversy over Cartwright's Puritanism swirled around the university. Receiving his B.A. in 1572, Browne remained in Cambridge until he was appointed to a teaching post in Stamford. Doubts over the proper form of the church troubled him greatly at this time. Driven out of Stamford by the plague in 1578, Browne returned by way of his home county to Cambridge. In nearby Dry Drayton the unordained Browne began preaching first to a conventicle in a home and then in the church of Puritan Richard Greenham. He was able to remain only a short time in the Cambridge area because of his denunciations of the not unsympathetic Archbishop Edmund Grindal.

At Norwich, in the Norfolk area unusually sympathetic to Puritanism, Browne became master of a hospital in 1580. Together with his Puritan colleague Robert Harrison (c. 1550-85), Browne began an independent congregation in Norwich, which grew to include fifty to a hundred persons. Twice imprisoned in London for his separation by the Norwich bishop, Browne (and Harrison) led forty persons into exile at Middelburg, the Netherlands, in

1582. Strife in the newly founded Middelburg congregation made Browne return to Scotland after a year with four or five other families, while Harrison remained in the Netherlands in charge of the congregation. Nevertheless, it was at Middelburg that Browne in 1582 issued his pioneering *Treatise of Reformation without Tarying for anie,* which was directed against Puritans who stayed within the Church of England. According to Browne, the only church in reality is a local body of experiential believers in Christ, united to him and to one another by a voluntary covenant. Such a church has Christ as its immediate head, is self-governing, and chooses a pastor, teacher, elders, and deacons according to the New Testament authorization. No church has authority over any other, but each owes helpfulness to the others.

In Scotland, Browne also encountered opposition to his anti-state church views, and after imprisonment there he returned to England again in 1584. Going to Holland once more, Browne arrived with a letter from Cartwright to Harrison seeking to have Separatists recognize the Church of England as a true church in spite of its defects. Browne then published a denial of Cartwright's arguments in England. Imprisoned once more because of that issue, Browne was released by the intervention of Lord Burghley, his relative in high places.

Wearying of the battle perhaps, the previously cantankerous Browne now agreed to conform to the Church of England, being allowed to teach in St. Olave's Latin school at Southwark, London, in 1586. By 1591 he had accepted ordination as an Anglican priest, serving for forty quiet years thereafter as Anglican rector at Achurch, Northamptonshire. He died there in prison in 1633, perhaps having become mentally ill.

Browne failed to maintain the querulous Separatism of his youth, eventually becoming little more than a participant in the prehistory of Congregationalism, especially since he did not stay with the tradition whose principles he pioneered in stating. Nevertheless, John Browne made a pioneer affirmation of Congregational principle and showed the way in practice toward a new way of church order. More than with any other person, the rather inaccurate title "Father of English Congregationalism" continues to be associated with troublesome Robert Browne.

2.
John
Robinson

John Robinson (c. 1578–1625), the European pastor of the Pilgrims, holds a secure place in the prehistory of Congregationalism.[37] Several important English Separatists preceded him. Henry Barrowe (1550?–93), while living at Norfolk, Cambridge, and London, wrote incisively as a lawyer favoring Separatism. Barrowe was imprisoned and hanged in 1593 with his ordained associate, John Greenwood, by order of Queen Elizabeth (1558–1603) for denying the queen's ecclesiastical supremacy. The Barrowist peculiarity in liturgy at that time was to deny validity to all forms of set prayers.

Barrowe and Greenwood won a number of followers, including Francis Johnson (1562–1618), who, after imprisonment, continued as pastor of the refugee congregation in Amsterdam, together with Henry Ainsworth (1571–1622), their teacher. In 1596 Johnson and Ainsworth published *A True Confession of Faith*, attacking the Church of England in forty-five articles. Johnson had two influential disciples, John Smyth (1554?–1612), the founding father of the modern Baptists, and John Robinson, pastor to the congregation at Leiden from which the Pilgrims emigrated to Massachusetts in 1620.

Originating at Gainsborough and Scrooby on the borders of Nottinghamshire, Yorkshire, and Lincolnshire, the original Pilgrim congregation with its successor in Leiden, the Netherlands, holds an honored place in American ecclesiastical history, even though the Pilgrims had not yet arrived at what became in America a normative non-Separatist position. A Separatist congregation was formed at Scrooby, Nottinghamshire, in 1606, with Richard Clyfton of nearby Babworth as pastor and William Brewster of Scrooby manor as presiding elder.[38] Also associated with the Scrooby congregation was the youthful William Bradford of Austerfield, two miles to the north, who later became the noted second governor of Plymouth Colony in the New World.

Most important of all was the teacher of the Scrooby congregation, John Robinson, who thereby completed the pattern of church organization acceptable to the Pilgrims, according to their interpretation of 1 Corinthians 12:28. Robinson was born in a nearby village, Sturton-le-Steeple, in 1578. Scanty information on his life indicates that he entered Corpus Christi College, Cambridge, in 1592. Obliged to resign his fellowship when he married his boyhood sweetheart, Bridget White of Sturton, Robinson appears to have become an Anglican priest at Mundham in Norfolk. He was suspended from his benefice there because of outspoken sermons. At St. Andrew's Church, Norwich, Robinson was appointed lecturer, a Puritan device for getting sympathetic ministers into parish pulpits. Deprived of his living at Norwich within a year or two after 1603 by the bishop, Robinson returned to the North, where he found his place as teacher of the Scrooby congregation.

Thus Robinson, a newly unemployed clergy deprived because of his faith, moved rapidly into Separatism, which he absorbed from his Puritan environment and, as he said, adopted because of the witness of the Holy Spirit from scripture compelling him toward separation: "Had not the truth been in my heart as a burning fire shut up in my bones, Jeremiah 20:9, I had never broken those bonds of flesh and blood, wherein I was so straitly tied."[39] Quickly Robinson found it necessary, with other Separatists, to emigrate to the Netherlands. He was with the second party from the Scrooby group going to Amsterdam (1608) and from there to Leiden (1609), where he became pastor of the Leiden congregation. For eleven years the Scrooby group lived in Leiden, relating also to Dutch and other churches there and being sustained by dialogues with William Ames, Robert Parker, and Henry Jacob, as they broadened their ecclesiology in a strange land.

With the door to their homeland closed, the Pilgrim group planned a third move, to the New World, because they wanted to preserve their own culture, escape the threat of war in Europe, and find a place where they could create a church after a New Testament pattern. Robinson enthusiastically supported plans for the move and is best known for his farewell sermon preached to the departing Pilgrims at Leiden, on July 21, 1620, challenging them to believe in the future, in the community they would build with God's guidance—a free church in a free commonwealth. He advised the adventurers not to "stick where Luther and Calvin left them," for he was confident that "the Lord had more truth and light yet to break forth out of his holy Word."

Robinson died five years later in Holland, reaching the New World only with his faith. Although he was a Separatist, Robinson did encourage stability with an increasingly irenic attitude, encouraging hearing of Episcopal sermons; but he still refused to participate in Anglican ordinances and sacramental communion. A comparison between Browne and Robinson may be helpful at this point. They were notably different in personality and leadership styles. Both were important in the difficult process of working out the theory and practice of Congregationalism. Browne was a pioneer of Separatism. Robinson was a practical formulator of the Independent-Congregational position, not quite having reached its ultimate non-Separatist position at the end of his life. Browne began as an innovative Separatist path-breaker but retreated under pressure of persecution from the startling implications of his new views. Robinson became a moderate, wise leader, open to new truths while actually nurturing developing congregations, and thereby, more than anyone else, directed Separatism into a realizable Independent-Congregational position to the right of the Baptists and slightly to the left of the Presbyterians. While an American perspective heightens the significance of Robinson because he was the Church Father of the Pilgrims and the inspirer of the *Mayflower* exodus-voyage, on the English scene, also, Robinson, more than anyone else, provided the transition between early Separatism and the dynamic position of Independent-Congregationalism, which became a strategic religious and political power center amid the turmoil of the civil war and Commonwealth England.

3.
William
Ames

William Ames (1576–1633) was *the* theologian of Puritanism and Reformed Pietism, the spiritual father of New England churches, a pioneer of covenant theology, a Ramist in educational method, a defender of high Calvinism against the Arminians, a polemicist against Roman Catholics, and a practical ethicist emphasizing Christian obedience to God's will. When Ames, in 1610, issued William Bradshaw's *English Puritanism* in a Latin version with a preface of his own, he not only recognized the importance of the term Puritan, but also made his own ecclesiastical statement of a principled independent, nonseparating Congregationalism.

William Ames was born at Ipswich, Suffolk, of a Puritan merchant family.[40] Educated at Christ's College, Cambridge, where he was tutored and greatly influenced by William Perkins, Ames might have become master of his college had he not shown Puritan traits. Prevented from seeking a pastorate at Colchester, Ames began an exile in the Netherlands in 1610 that lasted until his death in 1633. While serving as chaplain to the English governor at the Hague, Ames wrote controversially about the church in exchange with John Robinson and by 1615 had put together his own Congregational program: the congregation as an independent entity, the church covenant, ministers called by the individual congregations, and government and decision-making by the congregation itself. He also defended strict Calvinism against the libertarian Dutch Arminians and married the daughter of the previous English chaplain. Dismissed from his position, Ames attended the Synod of Dort in 1618 and 1619 as adviser to the Calvinists.

The English government prevented his appointment to an academic post in Leiden, where he wrote his famous *Medulla Theologiae*, a compendium of Calvinist theology, the "doctrine of living to God," for his theological students. Finally, he was made professor at the University of Franeker, in Friesland, in 1622, where he spent eleven productive years. He had hoped to go to New England, writing to John Winthrop in 1629, "I purpose therfor (God willing, and sending no hinderance beside what I yet know of) to come into England in sommer, and (upon the news of your safe arrivall, with good hope of prosperitie) to take the first convenient occasion of following after yow."[41] At the end of his life, after twenty-three years in the Low Countries, Ames left Franeker for Rotterdam, where he became an associate to Hugh Peter as minister at the English Puritan congregation. Plans there, supported by the city of Rotterdam, called for Ames to set up a Latin school-Puritan college, where he would teach. Barely two months after arriving in Rotterdam, Ames died from shock and exposure after the flooding of his house in 1633.

When explaining the theological significance of Ames, it is helpful to take note of three traditions within Reformed-Puritan theology: the analytic, the synthetic, and the Ramist reformed-empirical view, most clearly exemplified by Ames.[42] The Heidelberg Catechism of Ursinus and others pioneered in using analytical method. In an analytical catechism the basic question determines the whole structure. Not just the nature of humanity or of Christ's significance or even the end of human life (like Calvin) determines the structure of the Heidelberg Catechism, but rather the deep question "What is your only comfort in life and in death?" Humanity is at the center of the question, and the affinity to humanism is not an accident (at the same time, believing humanity is christologically rather than humanistically centered). This all roots in the self-discovery of humanism, in the ad hominem orientation of late medieval spiritual groups, and in the Protestant understanding of God's grace through Christ *pro me, pro nobis*. Everything is projected on the subject, yet the analysis of the same subject always follows from the objective. A strict systematic method results. In this sense, later Protestant orthodoxy, Lutheran as well as Reformed, is more Melanchthonian than it is the result of Luther's own method. Analytical theology was developed above all by a Danzig Reformed theologian, Bartolomäus Keckermann (1571–1609), who began his academic career teaching Hebrew in

Heidelberg.[43] Keckermann built his systematic theology on the Heidelberg Catechism, unfolding his *Systema Theologiae* in the second of two volumes, published in Geneva in 1614. A Reformed theologian basing his views on Melanchthon and Calvin, Keckermann used Aristotelian methods along with those of Duns Scotus, as developed by a Padua professor of philosophy and logic, Giacomo Zabarella (1532–89).[44] For Keckermann, theology is a practical discipline determined by its divine goal, *participatio Dei* or *ipsa salus*. This theology, Keckermann said, is wisdom rather than science, comparable to medicine.

The more typical catechisms, whether Roman Catholic or Luther's *Small Catechism,* were synthetic in nature, treating main points of doctrine one after another: Decalogue, Credo, Lord's Prayer, Baptism, Lord's Supper, and (not always) Penance. Synthetic catechisms, unlike the analytical ones, lacked systematic order, depending instead on the meaning of sacraments in a Christian's down-to-earth life, beginning, for example, with baptism. Another way of stating the nature of synthetic theological method is to emphasize a method proceeding from *causes* to effects (e.g., the Reformed method of Geneva, proceeding from divine predestination to its effects), over against the analytical method (Melanchthon and others), proceeding from *effects* to causes.[45] It has also been suggested that the reason Calvinism has been so preoccupied with questions of the subjective beginnings of faith was because it could not use the analytical method in regard to election.[46]

The Ramist-empirical method in theology was modeled most powerfully by William Ames. The analytical method bore little fruit on Reformed soil, despite the fact that it originated in Ursinus' Reformed effort to combat Lutheranism using Melanchthon's analytical method. The synthetic method fitted use of a strong doctrine of predestination, as in Zanchi and Beza. With its concern for the practice and use of doctrine, however, the Reformed faith was also attracted by an empirical-practical (Ramist) method as it had been used to a technical-practical, analytical method. The use of Ramism by Ames can be explained as follows. Peter Ramus (1515–72), a French humanist scholar and Reformed martyr, introduced an anti-scholastic, anti-Aristotelian method to Reformed theologians.[47] Calling itself a philosophy of experience, Ramism became, for a while, not only the dominant perspective at Heidelberg and its successor school, Herborn, but also flourished as a base for Puritan thought in old and new England. Intending to be practical, Ramism reduced logical arguments to simple disjunctive syllogisms. While lending itself to trivialization (and appropriation by modern, lineal, print-culture understandings), Ramism attempted theologically to avoid blurring the line between God and humanity so common to older Aristotelian approaches. It made sense especially to Puritans, that is, to English and German Calvinists who wanted to affirm a practical, empirical faith and to avoid extreme rationalism. The line of influence went directly from Ramus to William Perkins and especially William Ames, and from there to the Pilgrims and Puritans, famous in American colonial history. A word should be said in conclusion about the relation between Keckermann and Ramus. Although they opposed each other, the two Reformed theologians (the former Aristotelian and the latter anti-Aristotelian) were not so different as they thought. Both sought to make theology practical over against theoretical, both appealed to experience, both were analytical thinkers, and both depended on the Heidelberg Catechism. Whereas Ramus centered on the moment of subjective experience, Keckermann considered the goal that the experience reached.

Speaking more broadly, the following effects of Ames's work can be stated. Ames systematized the results of a religiously newly awakened Reformed Pietism. He sharply contested the liberal ethicizing of Reformed theology by the Arminians through his own method of casuistry in ethics. He reacted against scholastic rationalizing of the Reformed confession by using Ramist tools. He made use of a kind of Pietistic voluntarizing of religious confession of a Reformed type. Above all, Ames kept hold of the unity within Reformed faith, as he held on to the *objectivity* of Christian knowledge, while at the same time continuing to relate that knowledge to the *subjectivity* of Christian religious experience. Somewhat contradictory further developments were aided by the thought of Ames: humanism within Calvinism, the new empiricism, and the new Pietism, of which Ames was himself an example.

4.
Oliver
Cromwell

The final English representative of Puritanism, Oliver Cromwell (1599–1658), the first lay person and politician considered in this book, is by far the most significant person politically in our whole history, the only person in early modern English history to rank with the all-powerful Tudor and Stuart kings in power exercised.[48] Yet Cromwell, as a general and leader of a victorious revolution and later Lord Protector of England, was above all a man of religion and of Puritanism in particular. It is in light of this reality that I shall consider Oliver Cromwell.

Cromwell was the only son of a member of one of Queen Elizabeth's parliaments, a landlord and justice of the peace, who died when his son was eighteen. Having attended grammar school at Huntingdon, his hometown near Cambridge, Cromwell left Cambridge after a year to care for his widowed mother and is thought to have studied law with other country gentlemen at Lincoln's Inn, London. He then settled down to country living with his wife, five sons, and four daughters. Like others, he struggled in his early life with financial and spiritual difficulties and appears to have been convinced that he was "the chief of sinners" before his Puritan conversion, around age thirty.

Having become a member of Parliament, Cromwell struggled prominently as a Puritan in religion against King Charles I. When civil war began he rose rapidly to military leadership during the first civil war because of his newfound genius for organizing and inspiring light horse troops in the parliamentary armies. Having reorganized the New Model army during conflict between Parliament and the military in 1644, Cromwell won a decisive victory over the king. When Parliament and the army quarreled again, Cromwell supported his soldiers in a purge of Parliament and in the execution of Charles in 1649. He had no doubt that executing Charles was just: "A breach of trust ought to be punished more than any other crime whatever."

The Rump Parliament abolished monarchy and the House of Lords and declared England a commonwealth. But when the political situation worsened, the army made Cromwell Lord Protector. In that quasi-monarchical role, he had to compromise his ideal of representative government because he wished even more to rule a godly nation that would at the same time be religiously tolerant. Religious tolerance was still unusual when Cromwell advocated it.

Leaning toward religious independency (or Congregationalism), Cromwell was at the same time close to the radical Levellers, Diggers, and Fifth Monarchy Men, although he repudiated their anarchic extremes. His solution to the problem of religious division was a radical one for that age: he abandoned the state-church idea in favor of a national religion resting on Presbyterian, Independent, and Baptist bases. Although Cromwell unforgivably massacred the Irish as military commander in response to barbarous provocation, most of his contemporaries were horrified at the degree of tolerance Cromwell expressed! He fully acquiesced in the Puritan idea of providence expressed by the martyrologist John Foxe. As his letter to the speaker of the House of Commons shows, Cromwell regarded his civil war victory at Bristol in 1645 as a crusading result of a holy cause, under a righteous God.[49] And since he looked "unto providences," he was willing to trust whatever results history brought him. Like that of many who trust in external evidences of providence, the end of Cromwell's career was disappointing; yet the protectorate he built was religiously and politically tolerant. Cromwell had introduced the first modern revolution, integrating religion and politics. Puritan religion was at the heart of it.

Oliver Cromwell, apostle of toleration, grasped more power than any other commoner in English history and was rebuked by his Puritan colleague John Owen for flirting with the idea of becoming king. Sharing the Puritan doctrines of election and providence, Cromwell was ahead of his time in designing a church settlement without an Established Church and in readmitting the Jews to England in 1657. Overwhelmed by the return of the king and the Established Church, Cromwell's work nevertheless anticipated the time when the monarchy would be tamed by Parliament and dissenters would again be powerful and free. Although his personality was complex and flawed, his ultimate loyalty, in the best Puritan tradition, was to the "King of kings." Along with his great literary contemporary John Milton, Oliver Cromwell demonstrated the fruitfulness of the Congregational Way for the arts and politics, as well as for the life of the churches. A movement that produces leaders of such stature is worthy of renewed attention. If we forget the rich traditions nurtured by the Congregational Way in Puritan England, we are the poorer for it.

II.
American
Successors

Chapter Three
Puritan

1.
John
Cotton

Part II examines the fruits of European and English Protestant and Puritan teachings as they took root and flowered in the New World of colonial America. At this point it may be useful to refer to Darrett B. Rutman's definition of Puritanism: "a gift imparted by the preachers of the fellowship to the laypersons who heard them preaching."[50] A spiritual chronicle of Puritan ministerial generation goes as follows: Richard Rogers begat (spiritually) Paul Baynes, who begat Richard Sibbes, who begat John Cotton, who begat John Preston, who begat Thomas Shepard. I shall look especially at the fourth of those Puritan preachers, John Cotton, the most important Massachusetts Bay clergy.

The Pilgrim settlement at Plymouth, Massachusetts, preceded that at Boston by a decade. I described earlier how John Robinson fled with his Separatist English congregation to Leiden, the Netherlands, in order to find religious freedom. He encouraged them to migrate to the New World, preaching to the party of the departing Pilgrims, nearly half of his congregation, just before they sailed on the *Mayflower* in 1620, and he carried on a lively correspondence with "the church of God at Plymouth, New England." Although Robinson died in Leiden, his widow and two of his sons made the trip to the New World.

From Robinson and his successors comes our fuller definition of Congregationalism as the establishing of congregations called through an explicit church covenant, under Christ's leadership, to a creative mission of the Spirit. Through the church covenant,

Robinson argued in *Justification,* individual believers were built into a single edifice "united together in love as members of the body under the Head." In support of his views, Robinson cited five scriptural passages, four of which (Genesis 17:7, Leviticus 26:11–12, Revelation 1:11–13, and Hebrews 8:6) referred to the presence of God within a covenanted community and one of which (Matthew 18:17–20) was the Matthean rule for church discipline.[51]

Because Robinson did not accompany his flock to America, the Plymouth Pilgrims were without a regular minister for many years. A Separatist congregation could organize without a minister, however, and laypersons, such as William Brewster, their elder, served them in praise and prayer and in teaching the Bible and Christian doctrine.[52] A graduate of Cambridge University, Elder Brewster, as the only educated Pilgrim, was forced to preach, and he did it well. But he could not rightly administer the sacraments because he lacked ministerial ordination. No baptism or Lord's Supper was administered at Plymouth before 1629. Ordained ministers appeared briefly from time to time, but they were few, and there was no permanent minister until 1666, when John Cotton Jr. agreed to serve the Plymouth congregation. He remained as pastor for three decades. Thus the Pilgrims, like other groups in the Reformed, or Calvinist, tradition, oscillated between clerical and lay traditions of leadership.

The most important early leader at Plymouth was Governor William Bradford, much later described by Cotton Mather as the Moses who led his people to an English land of Canaan under the intimate guidance of God.[53] Like Brewster, Bradford was a member of the Scrooby congregation and had worked in exile as a weaver in Leiden. He sailed on the *Mayflower* in 1620 and was elected governor of Plymouth on the death of John Carver in 1621. Governor Bradford appointed the first day of Thanksgiving after the first harvest in the New World. He was reelected a dozen times, his last term ending in 1656. Bradford's administration covered hard years for the colony, which was saved through his skill in befriending the Indians. Bradford wrote *The History of Plymouth Plantation* (completed in 1650, published in 1850s), a historical masterpiece describing how God had providentially led the Pilgrims in the creation of their new society between 1620 and 1646.[54] Mather said that "the crown of all was Bradford's holy, prayerful, watchful and fruitful walk with God, wherein he was very exemplary."

As a Pilgrim, Bradford advocated separation from the state-controlled Anglican Church, but he exemplified the Puritan conscience, which believed that the civil government should support the true religion and choke off dissent. It was as yet too early for the characteristic American doctrine of the separation of church and state. In his own handwriting (on the back flyleaf of his personal copy of John Robinson's *Justification*), Bradford shows his dependence on his old pastor, Robinson, and on Peter Martyr Vermigli, a leading Reformed successor of John Calvin. To the question "Was it lawful for a magistrate to meddle in religion?" Bradford, citing Peter Martyr, wrote: "God commanded that the prince should have the book of the law and that both the tables were committed to the magistrate's power." "Even the heathen Aristotle knew that there was no greater virtue than religion and that the duty of the magistrate should not only 'provoke' his subjects into hearing the word of God 'but may inflict the same,' and he must use the civil power to insure that wicked and flagitious persons be neither taken into nor baptized into the church."[55]

While the Pilgrims, with their grit and pioneering commitment, were the heart of American Congregational beginnings, the Puritans, associated with future growth and economic success, were the force of the movement. Both groups, as products of the English Reformed tradition, refused to conform to the beliefs and practices of the Church of England, but the Puritans, unlike the Pilgrims, claimed that they did not wish to separate from the Church of England, only to purify it.

Until 1623 the Pilgrims had attempted to live communally with individuals working for the community, dividing all assets equally. Plymouth was small and poor; by 1667 the congregation had only 47 communicants. The town population was less than 350. Nearby Barnstable and Sandwich were also small towns with tiny churches. In contrast, thousands of Puritans had emigrated to the Massachusetts Bay area during the ten years following 1630, settling as independent farmers and artisans, so that New England grew from 500 to 10,000 inhabitants. Moreover, ordained ministers were plentiful among the Puritans, in contrast to the Pilgrims. Receiving a grant for New England territory as the Massachusetts Bay Company in 1629, the Puritans named their first village Salem. Captain John Endecott was chosen governor of the new plantation, while Francis Higginson and Samuel Skelton were elected pastor and teacher of the Salem church, which was gathered under a famous church covenant, based on scriptures.

In 1630 and 1631 other Puritans formed a new community and church at Charlestown and at Boston, which was to become the capital of New England. Governor John Winthrop came to be regarded by Cotton Mather, along with William Bradford, as a second Moses, leading the saints in Massachusetts.[56] More than any other person, Winthrop set the political and social character of the new colony, which molded the society of all New England. The charter for the Massachusetts colony extended the franchise to all citizen freemen who were members of the church, thus moving beyond English law and leading toward democracy. At the same time, Winthrop, like Bradford, was a strict Calvinist, who, in his *History of New England from 1630 to 1649,* noted down every-day incidents as well as colonial affairs, hoping that the facts would demonstrate that God's providence had always favored God's own people.

The first of the three first-generation Puritan leaders of New England was John Cotton (1584–1652), son of a lawyer in Derby, England. An excellent student at Cambridge, Cotton became one of only two later New Englanders to secure the B.D. degree, which required seven years of study beyond the M.A. degree. Associated with Cambridge Puritans, Cotton's rhetorical style was learned and ornate until his religious conversion by Richard Sibbes in 1609 enabled him to use the "plain" style of preaching. After ordination, Cotton became pastor of the important church of St. Botolph's, Boston, England, where he began to depart from the prayer book service. After spending twenty difficult, fruitful years there, Cotton at last was able to flee to New England, where new Boston, in 1633, received him enthusiastically as "teacher" of a newly formed congregation leaning (against Cotton's instincts) toward the Separatism of nearby Plymouth and Salem.

Cotton excellently exemplified Rutman's definition of Puritanism as a gift imparted by preachers to laypersons, since it was said of him in Boston that "whatever Cotton pronounced in the pulpit soon became either the law of the land or the practice of the church."[57] It was not literally true. Cotton's initial proposal for a secular code of laws patterned on the laws of Moses was rejected, yet his strong biblical direction of the commonwealth took hold. He was so thoroughly Reformed in doctrine that his trust in God's calling and justification of God's own people made him, like his follower Anne Hutchinson, distrust any preparation for salvation on the part of humanity. Along still another line, Cotton (according to Edmund Morgan's *Visible Saints*) originated on American soil the basic revivalist perspective that each church member must first experience a conscious "conversion."[58] These three religious tensions (biblical legalism, predestinarian rigor, personal conversion) would ultimately undo the New England Way! Indeed, the New

England confidence that it was God's people "set on a hill" can be taken as a unique case study of the glory and failure of that kind of Calvinistic conversionistic motif.

Cotton's lack of consistent support for Anne Hutchinson and especially his condemnation of the radical Calvinist Separationist and democrat Roger Williams (c. 1603–83) have made it difficult for modern people to understand or appreciate him. John Cotton jars us into the recognition that the Puritans did not intend to found the USA with its religious freedom, but rather were executing a less exciting flank attack on the Anglican hierarchy. Besides his nineteen volumes of sermons, seven of Cotton's leading works defended the New England Way, a church structure that he was the first to call Congregationalism. It is ironic that most of the few admirers of his ecclesiastical writings see in them the beginnings of democratic traditions that Cotton heartily hated! Preacher, Congregationalist, scholar—John Cotton (in Larzer Ziff's words) pieced together elements of Elizabeth's England and Moses' Israel into a pattern that never really came to exist in America, yet whose fragments are strewn throughout the course of American history.[59]

2.
Anne
Hutchinson

The second first-generation Puritan leader important for our story is Anne Hutchinson, the first significant woman in American history.[60] Daughter of a well-known English Puritan preacher, in 1591, Anne Marbury married a well-to-do merchant named William Hutchinson, to whom she bore fourteen children in twenty-two years. In 1633 her eldest son emigrated with John Cotton, whose preaching in England had attracted her also. She and the rest of her family came to New England in 1634, where learned, intelligent, and eloquent, she met on weekdays with women who repeated the substance of Cotton's sermons.

Turmoil arose when Hutchinson's theological distinctions between grace and works came to interfere with the personal standing of the Boston ministers and with the necessity for stability of a Puritan church already becoming established. It was plain to Anne Hutchinson that only John Cotton and John Wheelwright, her brother-in-law, were preaching a covenant of grace. The other Boston ministers, she said, were preaching a covenant of works. The situation was complicated by the similarity between John Cotton's theology and Anne Hutchinson's, as she had insisted. Both good Calvinist theologians, Cotton and Hutchinson were one in their common understanding of the inescapable personal character of the Protestant religious experience. No external evidences of righteousness were sufficient to reach the heart of their faith. At the same time, Cotton, the other ministers, and the magistrates were also beginning to promote the newer doctrine of humanity's preparation for grace as a way of controlling the organized church and community. Although he tried to help Hutchinson, Cotton, having fallen into an unstable political position, failed to stand his ground. The coming tragedy was precipitated by the inability of a male-dominated society to accept leadership from a powerful woman.

A majority of laypersons in the Boston church accepted Hutchinson's teachings, and the colony split into factions, especially when she was supported by Wheelwright and the young governor, Harry Vane. The other clergy and the magistrates believed that the existence of the whole enterprise was at stake. Led by John Winthrop and using clever tactics, they regained control of the government in 1637 and proceeded to disarm Anne's partisans and suppress her movement.

The theological accusation against Hutchinson was that she taught antinomianism (i.e., disregard for the moral law). While political and social reasons were important in the actions against her, her words and actions also triggered the fear of traditional Protestants of spiritual enthusiasm and private revelations. Twenty-five ministers met at Cambridge in the first synod of American Congregationalists, which condemned Anne Hutchinson for eighty-two errors after twenty-four days of painful hearings! She was then arraigned before the General Court, which accused her of disobeying the Fifth Commandment, commanding us to honor father and mother, including all in authority. Hutchinson responded that her authority came from Titus 2:3–4, where the elder women were instructed to teach the younger. The court responded with 1 Timothy 2:12, rejoicing when Paul said that no woman was to be permitted to teach. She responded, "It is said, I will poure my Spirit upon your Daughters, and they shall prophesie, etc. If God give mee a gift of Prophecy, I may use it."[61] She went on to speak of what appeared to be private revelations from the Holy Spirit, which damned her as an enthusiast in the eyes of the court.

Excommunicated from First Church in March 1638, John Cotton pronouncing sentence upon her, Anne Hutchinson was then banished from the colony by the court. With William Coddington and others, she bought the island of Aquidneck from the Indians in 1638, and settlements were made at Portsmouth and Newport, Rhode Island. After a century of turbulence these settlements coalesced with those of an earlier Separatist exile, Roger Williams, at Providence, and thus the state of Rhode Island was formed. After her husband's death in 1642, Hutchinson left Aquidneck and settled on some land in what is now Westchester County, New York.

There, in the next year, she was cruelly murdered with all her children but one. Some of the earliest Congregational churches in Rhode Island and New Hampshire resulted from Anne Hutchinson's inability to convince her fellow Bostonians of her theological soundness, and she produced an illustrious descendant, Thomas Hutchinson, the first great American historian and the last royal governor of Massachusetts, who was, ironically, a Tory and a conservative!

Anne Hutchinson's significance is still debated.[62] Although some defend Cotton and his associates for maintaining establishment conservatism against Hutchinson, others see her as an untimely pioneer of feminism or an eventually vindicated exemplar of religious freedom versus theological rigidity. There is no doubt some truth in both positions. Sacvan Berkovitch summarizes Anne's viewpoints favorably while noting their practical difficulties at the same time:

> The colonists, she charged, had substituted righteousness for redemption, social for christic conformity. She, too, . . . had heard the voice of John the Baptist predicting the fall of Antichrist. But as a saint she knew that she must attend *now* to the Baptist *within*. Avoiding the delusions of self, she would "see nothing, . . . have nothing, doe nothing, onely . . . stand still and waite" for the Holy Spirit to bring her, of its own accord . . . the millennium of the soul. That secured, she proceeded to instruct others: "Here is a great stirre about graces and looking to hearts (i.e., preparation), but give mee Christ, I seek not for (outward) graces but for Christ, . . . tell not mee of duties, but tell mee of Christ."[63]

Yet the New England Way was coherent, changing Cotton's thought away from Hutchinson's. Like her, his Christology diverged from Thomas Hooker's, emphasizing transformation, not preparation. Yet Cotton worked to harmonize extremes, becoming spokesperson for workable linkages between personal and corporate piety in a successful state. According to this reading, Anne Hutchinson may well have been ahead of her time in envisaging a freer relationship between religion and society than seventeenth-century Puritans thought possible.

3.
Thomas
Hooker

The third of the New England pioneers considered here, Thomas Hooker (1586–1647), helped to found the state of Connecticut and became the most eloquent preacher of first-generation Puritans.[64] After graduation from Puritan Cambridge, Hooker became chaplain to the Drake family in Esher, Surrey, where he effected a spiritual cure for the depressed Mrs. Drake, who died happily in 1625. No doubt that experience as spiritual counselor had a lasting effect on Hooker's ministry regarding the experience of preparation for grace.[65] Hooker became the most effective spiritual leader among early Puritans. The missionary John Eliot described the atmosphere of Hooker's house in England as follows: "Here the Lord said unto my dead soul—Live! And through the grace of Christ I do live, and I shall live forever. When I came to this blessed family I then saw as never before the power of godliness in its lively vigor and efficacy."[66]

Silenced in England by Bishop Laud, Hooker fled to Holland, where he served two years as minister to an English congregation at Delft and then as colleague of William Ames at Rotterdam. While in Holland, Hooker perfected his Puritan ecclesiology together with John Davenport, later founder of New Haven, and Hugh Peter, later pastor at Salem, as members of the short-lived English Congregational Classis in the Netherlands. He was also a friend of John Cotton: Hooker, Cotton, and Samuel Stone arrived together in 1633 at Boston on the same ship.[67] The Massachusetts people were delighted, saying they now "had Cotton for their clothing, Hooker for their fishing, and Stone for their building."

Hooker was welcomed to Newtowne (Cambridge) by a group of his English followers who had already emigrated, awaiting his arrival. Hooker and Stone were chosen pastor and teacher at Newtowne, where Hooker soon became prominent. He was called on to answer the Separatist Puritan Roger Williams in debate, and he rebuked Governor Endecott for cutting the cross out of the English national flag. The congregation prospered, and one of its members was elected governor in 1635, but it desired more freedom and, beginning a familiar American activity, desired to move toward the frontier, namely Connecticut.

This move was accomplished in 1636, despite the opposition of John Cotton in Boston and the General Court: Hartford was founded, and Hooker at once became leader of the state. Hooker led one hundred members of his Cambridge congregation on a trek into the wilderness of the Connecticut River valley to Hartford, guiding 160 head of cattle and sending the furniture and supplies around by water. Other Massachusetts churches migrated also, the first-comers being followed by others from Dorchester, Watertown, and Roxbury. By the next May, 800 persons were living at Windsor, Hartford, and Wethersfield, Connecticut, with the settlement at Springfield coming later. While Hooker at Hartford appeared to be more democratic than Massachusetts in relating voting qualifications to property rather than to church membership, he was one with Cotton in trying to keep church membership standards as high as possible. Rather than emphasizing Hooker's democratic or political interests, contemporary scholars believe that Hooker is better understood as a pastoral leader, and that the primary motives for migrating to Connecticut were to escape Bay Colony disputes and build a purer congregation.

Thomas Hooker exerted a more vigorous rhetorical influence on American Puritanism than did his leadership equal and colleague, the gentle intellectual John Cotton. Cotton's poetic eulogy of Hooker reveals the rather low Christology of the Puritans and their sense of continuity with the Catholic Church:

> To see three things was holy Austin's wish,
> Rome in her Flower, Christ Jesus in the Flesh,
> And Paul i' the Pulpit; lately men might see,
> Two first, and more, in Hooker's Ministry.
>
> Zion in Beauty, is a fairer sight,
> Than Rome in Flower, and all her Glory dight:

Yet Zion's Beauty did most clearly shine,
In Hooker's Rule, and Doctrine; both Divine.

Christ in the Spirit, is more than Christ in Flesh,
Our Souls to quicken, and our States to bless:
Yet Christ in Spirit brake forth mightily,
In Faithful Hooker's searching Ministry.

Paul in the Pulpit, Hooker could not reach,
Yet did He Christ in Spirit so lively Preach:
That living Hearers thought He did inherit
A double Portion of Paul's lively spirit. . . .

'Twas of Geneva's Worthies said, with wonder,
(Those Worthies Three:) Farell was wont to thunder;
Viret, like Rain, on tender grass to shower,
But Calvin, lively Oracles to pour.

All these in Hooker's spirit did remain:
A Son of Thunder, and a Shower of Rain,
A pourer forth of lively Oracles,
In saving souls, the sum of miracles.[68]

Sargent Bush suggests that Hooker's intense, meditative piety helped to create the questing pilgrim type in American literature, apparent in Cooper's Leatherstocking, Melville's Ishmael, Whitman's Self, and Twain's Huckleberry Finn.[69] Cotton's place in American history is secure. Anne Hutchinson, cast out "as a Leper, a Hethen and a Publican," accompanied by Mary Dyer, later hanged for her Quaker faith on Boston Common, could only say for herself in departing, "Better to be cast out of the Church than to deny Christ."[70] Perhaps the reality of her witness outweighs the more impressive rhetoric of her Puritan antagonists and colleagues.

4.
Harriet
Beecher
Stowe

The second woman in our Puritan story, Harriet Beecher Stowe (1811–96), was perhaps, more than any other single person, the precipitator of the great Civil War, as well as a fine example of how Puritanism declined in the nineteenth century and was displaced by a new gospel of social service, of women's rights, and of anti-slavery ferment. An encounter took place in 1863 between President Abraham Lincoln, who had just emancipated the slaves, and the notorious author of *Uncle Tom's Cabin*. As they shook hands, Lincoln is supposed to have said, "So this is the little lady who made this big war."[71]

Harriet Beecher was born in New England, one of eleven notable children of the preacher Lyman Beecher. She was first a pupil and then a teacher in her sister's school in Hartford and, after 1832, at Cincinnati, where her father headed Lane Theological Seminary. Like most of his children, Lyman Beecher passed through a period of hard struggle and poverty. He left Yale a Calvinist and a believer in religious revivals; his wives and children, by their common sense and reactions to the sorrows of life, helped to humanize his views.[72] As a young pastor, he became renowned for his outspoken attacks on dueling, intemperance, and infidelity. At Lane he fought conservative bigotry and, with his family, became aware of the evils of slavery.

Her father described her at seven as a genius, but she reached middle life, apparently worn out by childbearing, poverty, and domestic drudgery, before the genius was revealed. Her marriage to a widowed seminary professor, Calvin Ellis Stowe, in 1836, aided her intellectual development. Calvin Stowe opposed doctrinal controversy and rejected dogmatic New England theology in favor of the mediating theology of German Pietists, especially Friedrich Tholuck. Harriet Beecher Stowe fought against predestination, favoring, as did her husband, a more optimistic trust in the union of the soul with God. She lived for eighteen difficult years in Cincinnati, separated only by the Ohio River from a slaveholding community and coming to know well the tragedy of slavery for ordinary persons.

After her husband became professor at Bowdoin College in Maine in 1850, she decided to write a story to awaken the nation to the evils of the Fugitive Slave Act (and to augment her husband's meager salary). Published first in installments in a tiny anti-slavery paper, *Uncle Tom's Cabin,* as a book, became one of the greatest publishing successes in history. By the end of its first year, 1852, 300,000 copies had been sold in the United States and a million and a half copies in Great Britain and its colonies. *Uncle Tom's Cabin* succeeded because its crusading author was the first American realist of any consequence and the first to use fiction for a profound criticism of American society, especially its failure to live up to the promises of democracy. Although she was at times sentimental, she possessed an acute New England conscience, a Puritan capacity to face evil, and the power to give dramatic form to a welter of emotions.

Besides her unsurpassed role in crusading against slavery, Harriet Beecher Stowe also advocated women's rights. In *Agnes of Sorrento* and elsewhere, she advocated the sacred role of women in Christianity. She believed that women were intended by God to minister, equally with men, to fellow seekers, and that this was proved by the scriptures themselves, in their revelation of a female prophetic tradition.[73] Her book *Woman in Sacred History* presented character sketches of historic women who had been anointed to speak for God. Finally, in her devotional manual, *Footsteps of the Master,* she presented her unusual theological interpretation that not only did Christ partake of human nature through the incarnation, but also that his humanity was distinctly feminine. She also recovered Mariology in the land of the Puritans! There is no evidence that Stowe was acquainted with Antoinette Brown, the first woman officially ordained in 1853, at Butler, New York, but their viewpoints were the same. By 1921, when Antoinette Brown died, at age ninety-six, 3,000 women ministers were serving the church in America. Thus, the viewpoints of the pioneers came gradually to prevail.

Unlike *The Scarlet Letter, Moby Dick*, and *Huckleberry Finn, Uncle Tom's Cabin* was a plea for a cause, a book with a mission, and once the mission—abolition—was achieved, it became a historic landmark. Here Harriet Beecher Stowe was still a Puritan: the moral subverted the art. Social and religious motives fueled her fervor but also overheated her imagination. But that was why her work was popular: people were not only moved, but also edified. Marie Caskey has summarized the religion of Stowe as follows:

> The religion of Harriet Beecher Stowe [centered in] "the enthusiasm of love." It was not the "disinterested benevolence" of Samuel Hopkins, or even the millennial ardor of her father, but a domesticized, highly personal vision of a love between a gentle Jesus and his children, his brothers, and his sisters. Mrs. Stowe's theology was liberal and Christ-centered, but compared to her brother Henry's, it was also more akin to the evangelicalism of Lyman Beecher's generation.[74]

In the Beecher family history, one may observe how early Puritanism came eventually to be reshaped into a personal, more individual, more optimistic, and, at times, oversentimental form. Thus, one can observe the transition into some of the familiar nineteenth- and twentieth-century ways of relating religion and culture. That transition may be further clarified by showing how, in the eighteenth century, another tradition of Pietism, Revivalism, and Evangelicalism (along with Enlightenment) entered into American life, as Revivalism (and the reactions against it) ushered Puritanism into an intermediate stage.

Chapter Four
Pietist

This chapter considers a second major component of UCC religious typology: Pietism. Although nationally speaking, Puritanism is associated with the criticisms of the state church by English people, and Pietism with oppositional views over against the German state churches, their typological similarities suggest that they were really part of the same movement. It is usually said that Pietism encouraged a more individualistic attitude,[75] while Puritans consistently maintained socially responsible actions toward the state and the community, inherited from medieval Catholicism and having taken on new life through Reformation teachings. Differences that exist between communal and individual perspectives no doubt have something to do with contrasted attitudes and political realities in England and Germany, respectively, as well as the fact that greater individualism had appeared generally after 1675, when Pietism began, while the century-older Puritan movement grew out of a more communal society.

A sketch of Puritan and Pietist characteristics shows how much they had in common. A recent American historian of Pietism, F. Ernest Stoeffler, believes that Puritans manifested four elements.[76] What the Puritans aimed for, Stoeffler argued, were purer forms of worship, more church discipline, separation from established churches, and greater preciseness or heightened piety. Stoeffler then described Pietists as having the following characteristics: religious idealism (comparable to Puritan desires for purer worship forms), a strong biblical emphasis (similar to Puritan demands for more church discipline), an oppositional orientation (similar to but not as extreme as the Puritan demand for separation from established churches), and an insistence that the individual become personally related to God (similar to the more general statement of Puritans seeking greater preciseness or heightened piety).[77]

Additional recent literature studying both movements tends to find many similarities and actual interrelationships. For example, August Lang attempted, in a German essay of 1941, to establish connections between Puritans and Pietists from the sixteenth-century German Bucer to the eighteenth-century English Wesleys.[78] As I have noted previously, Lang regarded the German Bucer as the first Puritan and William Perkins, an Englishman as the first Pietist! German historian Martin Schmidt claimed that Stoeffler's definition of Pietism as "experimental religion" lacks completeness, and Schmidt wished to specify that the Pietist conception of rebirth meant that Pietists wished to change the world by changing people.[79] The German Johannes Wallmann developed a twofold way of describing the beginnings of Pietism. He claimed that it was both a personal movement of piety (with the German Johann Arndt as its founder) and a social movement encouraging new forms of churchly community life, especially using small groups (with another German Lutheran, Philipp Jacob Spener, as its founder).[80] Finally, the German Hartmut Lehmann insisted that theological and social similarities between Puritanism in England, Catholic Jansenism in France, and Pietism in Germany were nevertheless phased differently in time, and therefore separately describable. All three developed in different historical situations but from the beginning reached similar social groups, presumably the middle more than the lower classes. In each case, according to Lehmann, many clerical leaders came to oppose lifeless church leadership as well as excessive dependence on an increasingly secularized state, and sensitive people responded to their programs.[81] At any rate, evidence for mutual relations between Puritans and Pietists were much more common and fruitful than is generally known, not least of all in the New World, at this time rapidly emerging out of its original colonial isolation.

1.
Cotton
Mather

The external details of his life are rather undramatic. Cotton Mather (1663–1728) was the son of Increase Mather and the grandson of the noted John Cotton. Entering the ministry after Harvard in 1685, he succeeded his father at Second Church in Boston and, like his father, became the leading cleric in the Massachusetts Bay Colony.[82] Cotton Mather played an important role in the Salem witchcraft trials, having helped to initiate them with his *Memorable Providences Relating to Witchcraft* (1689), but he later criticized "spectral evidence" and executions. Although he never traveled, his reputation spread abroad through his writings and scientific papers, the British Royal Society electing him a member in 1713. No other American has published so much as Cotton Mather: 444 books and fifteen unpublished manuscripts. His greatest work was a rambling history, the *Magnalia Christi Americana* (1702), and his *Bonifacius* (1710) (Essays to Do Good) became a moral handbook for Americans. Politically ineffective, Mather continued to guide church affairs through his days, although conflicts and disappointments made life difficult for the ascetic, hardworking cleric.

Of all the Puritans, Cotton Mather displayed the most fully developed Pietistic emphases in his life, in his writings, and in personal relationship to A.H. Francke, the German Lutheran leader of Pietism.[83] Robert G. Pope has summarized Mather's life as a Pietist:

In the Puritan divine, prostrate on the floor of his study, pleading his own vileness, lies the core of [Cotton Mather], the man. . . . He established an extraordinary religious regimen. Six times daily he interrupted his affairs for worship and meditation; twice each month he forced himself through a sleepless vigil of self-examination; fasting became a routine part of his religious observations. . . . He drew from this brooding introspection to create the new pietism he increasingly endorsed after 1710 and made explicit in *Bonifacius* (1710). Pietism became his vehicle for revitalizing New England's religious life: it offered men an affective belief in Christ, it cut through sectarian divisions, and it countered the Arminian drift of the times. Mather's pietistic organization would engage men against the evils of society and accomplish the reformation which two generations of New England clergy had unsuccessfully sought.[84]

From the beginning of his ministry, Cotton Mather was a thorough Pietist. David Levin rejects the Perry Miller thesis that Mather stopped preaching jeremiad sermons after the clergy lost political power early in the eighteenth century, resorting instead to Pietistic instructions for reforming communal life and making use of voluntary associations instead of politics. In his *Small Offers . . . unto the Designs of Practical Godliness* (1689), Mather warned busy Bostonians that God would "find an Eternity to Damn the man that cannot find a Time to Pray."[85] By 1709 and 1710 Mather had begun to speak of "American Pietism." He wrote in his "Diary": "I represented, the Methods of *Piety* proposed in these Essayes, as being the true *American Pietism*. I considered that the People who are shortly to be the *Stone cutt out of the Mountain,* will be a People of these Principles. . . . I shall also endeavour to send these things unto Dr. *Franckius* in *Saxony.*"[86]

Cotton Mather had become acquainted with Francke's reports from the Halle orphan asylum because his diary entries for March 12 and 13, 1711, show that he not only sent to Francke an account of his work on the foundation of an orphan asylum in Boston built after the Halle model, but also a present of gold.[87] In November, Mather sent another gold gift to the Halle orphan house and indicated that he planned to translate some English devotional books into German. Cotton Mather published Francke's lengthy letter of thanks for the gift under the title, *Nuncia Bona . . . A Brief Account of Some Good & Great Things A DOING For the Kingdom of GOD in the Midst of EUROPE* (1715).[88]

Mather's letter included fulsome praise for A.H. Francke's work near Halle, Germany. Francke's orphanage supported 500 children, his German school had 1,600 scholars, and his Latin, Greek, and Hebrew school had 300 students, not to speak of the school for noblemen and for women, a hospital, a printing press, a university, and a divinity school totaling more than 3,000 students. Mather said the following about Francke:

> That which lies at the bottom of all this Great Man's Designs, is, to advance *True, Real, Vital Piety*. . . . [The Halle University] is one of the most flourishing in the World, having in it more than Three Thousand of Students, resorting from all Parts of *Europe* unto it. Here still PIETY is the main Concern; and the Students are not sent forth . . . until it appear . . . that they know what it is to *Live unto God*. . . . And you will be for the uniting of Councils with Good men, upon the Noble Intentions of a *Bonifacius*.[89]

Rather than teaching moralism in the *Bonifacius*, Mather's intention was to be an instrument of piety in one's doing good.

Another element in Mather's Pietistic faith was his distinctive view of eschatology. Hartmut Lehmann regards eschatology as essential to Pietists, who believed that true Christians were persecuted in their time but that it was God's plan to save them in the not-too-distant future by the return of Christ.[90] The unusual nature of Cotton Mather's eschatology was his combination of ardent chiliasm (Christ is coming soon) with an optimistic spirit of ecumenical renewal and activist reform of the church and society, helping to lay the groundwork for the Great Awakening after his death.[91] Although he changed his mind later, Mather believed that the Jewish people would be converted before the coming of Christ, laboring himself toward that end. In his mission tract *India Christiana* (1721), Mather also anticipated the liberation of Negro slaves: "Then should we see the Africans no longer treated like meer Beasts of Burden, as they are in the Plantations of cruel Americans."[92]

In summary, Cotton Mather, in spite of the way his introspective egocentricity displeases people, remained firmly within the tradition of Puritan spirituality going back to John Cotton and Thomas Hooker. He even leaned healthily toward Anne Hutchinson's forbidden confidence in direct spiritual assurance. At the same time, Mather, through his consistent Pietist methods and tendencies, was unwittingly fanning the spark in New England that would burst into the flames of the Great Awakening a few years after his death in Jonathan Edwards' Northampton church.

In the words of Richard Lovelace:

> During the seventeenth century the Puritan and Pietist evangelical strains noted, admired, and cross-pollinated one another. . . . The interrelationships during the Great Awakening between Zinzendorf's Lutheran Pietism, Wesleyan Arminianism, and the Puritan Calvinism of Whitefield, Edwards, and the Tennents was a later instance of the same sort. . . . The vitality of the Evangelical Movement ebbed during the late nineteenth and early twentieth centuries, as its center declined into Fundamentalism, relinquishing the ecumenical and social initiatives cherished by Mather and Francke. . . . But fortunately the ideals of biblical doctrine, godly living, unity, evangelistic mission, and social compassion held by these men have constantly been upheld in one segment of the church or another.[93]

2.
Michael
Schlatter

Michael Schlatter (1716–90), a pioneer founder of the German Reformed Church in America, is the first representative being considered of what later became the Evangelical and Reformed constituency of the UCC.[94] Like Cotton Mather, Schlatter was a moderate churchly, confessional Pietist. His career can best be described as an outgrowth of the Pietism he learned in his home city of St. Gall, Switzerland, near where the Reformed Church was born. The Congregational and Reformed leaders differed from one another. Mather's literary accomplishments came out of a third-generation setting in a homogeneous church and community. A half-century later Schlatter organized a first-generation non-English-speaking church in Penn's colony that guaranteed a rather chaotic religious toleration, rather than manifesting the tighter aspects of the Puritan Way. Pietism thus took on different forms in Massachusetts and Pennsylvania, especially since Schlatter, unlike Mather, had to deal also with the new religious excitement known as the Great Awakening.[95]

The Great Awakening imported English Evangelical and Continental Pietist innovations in religious thought and practice, communicating them fairly successfully throughout the colonies. Great Awakening influences were muted among the Germans in Pennsylvania because religion among first-generation immigrants remained chaotic. Three forms of Pietism emerged. One was *sectarian* Pietism, especially as practiced by the Seventh-Day Dunkers at Ephrata. Conrad Beissel, in the 1730s, had formed a hypersectarian Protestant monastic community after separating his Pietist converts from the Reformed and the sectarian Dunker-Brethren-Baptists. Moravian missionaries, especially the powerful Count von Zinzendorf, tried to draw all Christians into a second, *ecumenical* form of Pietism after 1741 with his Unionist "tropes." The main impact of the Great Awakening in Pennsylvania derived from George Whitefield's visit in 1740. Then, a little later, came *confessional* Pietism among the Germans, as the European immigrant Lutheran and Reformed leaders, Henry M. Mühlenberg and Michael Schlatter, sought to deepen the spirituality and organizational forms of their own people and tried to safeguard them from what was regarded as dangerous sectarian and ecumenical Pietism.[96]

About a century after Congregationalists and Anglicans began arriving in the New World, the first significant numbers of Swiss and German immigrants came from Bern, Zurich, and the Palatinate region of Germany to the Carolinas, Virginia, Maryland, New Jersey, and New York, and especially Pennsylvania. These immigrants were poor, many having paid for passage by becoming redemptioners (legally obligated servants), but they had a high rate of literacy—76.1 percent for males over sixteen.[97] Arriving without food, medicine, or money, the Germans brought along Bibles, prayer books, and catechisms, which allowed the mothers and fathers to become teachers of the young. Laypersons were pressed into service to give religious instruction to children, who had formerly been educated in parochial schools attached to Reformed churches in home villages.

It was logical that the first twelve regularly organized German Reformed churches in the New World were started by a lay immigrant schoolteacher, John Philipp Boehm (1683-1749).[98] Theologically trained immigrant Reformed clergy were not always as interested in forming churches as was the practical schoolteacher Boehm, who was ordained later. For example, the Rev. Samuel Güldin (1660–1745), a Swiss Pietist, had been dismissed from his Bern pastorate for associating in religious societies with non-Reformed believers, before arriving at Philadelphia in 1710.[99] Fighting for individual rebirth and against preoccupation with denominational organization, Güldin preached occasionally at Germantown but made no effort to organize Reformed churches.

After Boehm, Michael Schlatter was the most effective organizer of German Reformed churches in colonial America. Born in 1716 at St. Gall, Schlatter was the son of a bookkeeper and a member of an honored family loyal to the Reformed Church and participating in civic offices. Young Schlatter's pastor was Christof Stähelin (1665–1727), the father of St. Gall Pietism, who had widely influenced Swiss Pietism through the publication of his brief catechism, *The Conjugal Yes*, based on the *Halleluja* of Theodor UnderEyck (1635–93).[100] A German from Duisburg, UnderEyck studied theology in the Netherlands under Voetius at Utrecht and under Coccejus at Leiden, thus combining the federal or covenant theology with the spirit of Voetian Pietism. His books cited Perkins, Ames, Bayly, Baxter, and others frequently, another indication of converging Puritanism and Pietism. Stähelin published a volume of selections from UnderEyck's 1678 *Halleluja* in Bern in 1719 with the title *Ehliches Ja-Wort*.[101]

Like UnderEyck, whose *Christi Braut* (1670) supported his devotional meditations with references to the Heidelberg Catechism, Stähelin's *Catechetischer Hausz-Schatz* (Basel, 1724) took nearly a thousand pages to discuss every question of the Heidelberg Catechism devotionally.[102] It became a Pietistic classic and was brought to Pennsylvania by Swiss and German Reformed people. Described as the "St. Gall Spener," Stähelin was forbidden to preach after a young woman fainted during his 1715 Pentecost sermons.[103] The Swiss effort to forbid Pietist conventicles contributed to the emigration of Mennonites and perhaps others to colonial America.

A wandering, erratic ministerial student, Michael Schlatter studied in both Switzerland and Holland. In 1746 the South Holland Synod (with the aid of the Heidelberg, Germany, church consistory) deputized young Schlatter to go to America to "organize the ministers and congregations [of the German Reformed Church] into a coetus," an administrative synodical body subordinate to the Dutch synods. A whirlwind of activity by Schlatter followed. By the summer of 1747, after a year in America, Schlatter had visited, surveyed, and analyzed the forty-six weak and disparate Reformed congregations. He had gained the confidence of the other four active Reformed pastors and was able to organize an annual coetus for mutual examination, strengthening, and planning by the pastors and their elders. Thus Schlatter organized the Reformed Church in the Pennsylvania field. He also served as pastor of the Philadelphia (Pennsylvania) church known today as Old First Reformed Church, United Church of Christ, founded in 1727.

Between 1754 and 1757 Schlatter collected $60,000 in Europe and became administrator of the resulting charity schools for German immigrants. He brought along back to Pennsylvania six new ministerial recruits, including the Rev. Philip William Otterbein

(1726–1813), a strict Pietist from Herborn, Germany, who later founded the United Brethren Church, which finally merged in 1968 into the United Methodist Church. From the German Reformed standpoint, Otterbein became an example of the dangers of Separatist Pietism. The charity schools failed because the German immigrants feared an anglicizing process. Schlatter bore the brunt of unfavorable publicity, losing his standing as a Reformed clergy and ending his career as a British and American army chaplain and a retired landowner. The last thirty years of Schlatter's life were regrettably anticlimactic. Probably thinking himself to have been a failure when he died in 1790, Schlatter was, in reality, a notable Pietist and a good organizer who deserves to be remembered with affection and respect. Like Cotton Mather, who also failed to accomplish all his religious ideals, Michael Schlatter represented a fruitful convergence of Puritan and Pietist faiths and life-styles.

3.
Jonathan
Edwards

Of all the Americans in our UCC story, Jonathan Edwards (1703–58) is regarded as the greatest theologian and is unique as stimulator of the religious revival known as the Great Awakening (1740–42).[104] Born in Connecticut, son of a pious Puritan clergy, Edwards graduated from the new Yale College in 1720, returning to Yale as tutor after a short Presbyterian pastorate in New York. In 1726 he became pastoral associate and then successor to his aging maternal grandfather, Solomon Stoddard, at Northampton, Massachusetts. Edwards married the equally pious Sarah Pierrepont of New Haven, and they had eleven children.

Experiencing a new grasp of God's glory and excellence while a graduate student, Edwards' own preaching became an instrument of "surprising conversions" at Northampton in the 1730s. Having welcomed the great English itinerant preacher George Whitefield to Northampton in the 1740s, Edwards examined Revivalism appreciatively and critically in his *Treatise on Religious Affections*.[105] Also at Northampton, Edwards was dismissed by his congregation for insisting that a personal profession of faith be necessary for full church communion. He found refuge in 1751 at a frontier church in Stockbridge, Massachusetts, as missionary to the Indians and pastor and found time also to write his treatises on *Freedom of the Will, Original Sin, The Nature of True Virtue,* and *The End for Which God Created the World.* Chosen by the newly founded College of New Jersey (Princeton) as president, Edwards died of a smallpox inoculation at the age of fifty-four, only a few weeks after assuming office. Like many other Puritans, the inner life of Jonathan Edwards was more dramatic than the external events of his career.

One historian has sorted out five aspects of the thought of Edwards, making understanding of the whole person difficult: He was a Puritan exegetical preacher; a New England polemicist taking up specific problems of revivals and church order; an apologist for strict Reformed doctrine and "New Light" experientialism over against enlightened reasonableness; a Christian ontologist enraptured of Being in general; and a sacred historian beholding events leading from the creation to times of millennial expectation.[106] The second and third aspects show how much Edwards was part of what we have been calling "Pietism." In his *Religious Affections* (1746), Edwards insisted, against the revival critics' ideal of sober, "reasonable" religion, that "the essence of all true religion lies in holy love," a love proving its genuineness by its inner quality and practical results. In 1749 Edwards edited the memoirs of his son-in-law, David Brainerd, a Revivalist missionary to the Indians. Two years earlier Edwards had written in support of a proposed international "concert of prayer" for "the Revival of Religion and the Advancement of Christ's Kingdom on Earth," arguing that the worst of the great tribulations prophesied in the book of Revelation as preceding the millennium were already past and that the church could look forward to an increasing success of the gospel among people. Thus Edwards advocated a postmillennial position looking for triumphant expansion of a reforming church before a literal thousand years under the personal reign of Christ. While his viewpoint resembled later secularized progress doctrines, Edwards thought of himself as clearly within the Puritan or Pietist spiritual awakening tradition for which he fought so valiantly. Edwards remained within the older Reformation-Calvinist revival mold, using an Old Testament theocratic model. Later, revival tradition shifted to a nontheocratic tradition drawn from the awakening of the church in Acts.[107]

For a century after his death, Edwards' influence on American and English Protestantism was marked. After the Civil War his prestige declined and he was remembered mainly as a hell-fire preacher and abstruse metaphysician. After the 1930s Edwards was rediscovered by theologians reacting against liberalism and by secular scholars seeking to describe the American mind. Thomas A. Schafer summarizes well a contemporary scholarly view of Edwards:

> Edwards' ability to combine religious intensity with intellectual rigor and moral earnestness, the cosmic sweep of his

theological vision, his emphasis on faith as an "existential" response to reality, his insistence that love is the heart of religion, and his uncompromising stand against all forms of idolatry are some of the reasons his life and writings are again being seriously studied.[108]

Additional reference to Edwards' own conversion and to the revival at Northampton will help to make more vivid the intensely Pietistic tone of his ministry. At age seventeen his conversion occurred, and Edwards later described it as follows:

> I walked abroad alone, in a solitary place in my father's pasture, for contemplation. And as I was walking there, and looking up on the sky and clouds, there came into my mind so sweet a sense of the glorious majesty and grace of God, that I know not how to express. I seemed to see them both in a sweet conjunction; majesty and meekness joined together.[109]

That experience of Edwards resembles the conversion of Augustine of Hippo 1,300 years earlier and is a fine example of the "twice-born" religious mentality that William James examined. At the same time, Edwards appreciated the stability and order of "once-born" Christian life that was more familiar to some of his contemporaries.

The Northampton revival followed an effective series of sermons by Edwards on "Justification by Faith," late in 1734. Sudden and violent conversions followed, notably on the part of a young woman of the town who had been one of the greatest "company-keepers." Throughout the winter and spring Edwards led the most spectacular revival that New England had yet seen. More than 300 persons were seized on, and almost the whole town became communicants. Strife, backbiting, and gossip disappeared. The suicide of his uncle by marriage, the merchant Joseph Hawley, in May 1735 commenced a reaction, and by the end of the year the revival was over, the town not knowing quite what had happened and remembering with mixed feelings the ecstasies of the first months. Thus a peculiar American tradition, Revivalism, had its beginnings in New England.

In conclusion, a question arises whether the road that Edwards took toward religious *symbolism* (over against the more common American road toward religious *moralism*) has not led to sentimental, self-righteous attitudes, found in present-day religious thought, which often evidences lack of passion for eliminating specific social evils.[110] Although Edwards (and Horace Bushell after him) may be criticized this way, moralism is also part of the problem for Americans. Moreover, it is truer to Edwards and to the Puritan-Pietist traditions of the UCC, to see in his *Nature of True Virtue* a profoundly responsible attitude, revering both "benevolence to Being in general" and "disinterested benevolence," the famous doctrine of Edwards' disciple Samuel Hopkins. Edwards wrote: "Virtue is the beauty of those qualities and acts of mind, that are of a *moral* nature. . . . And therefore when we are inquiring concerning the nature of true virtue, viz., wherein this true and general beauty of the heart does essentially consist—this is my answer to the inquiry: True virtue most essentially consists in benevolence to Being in general."[111] Possibly anticipating a sentimental watering down of his doctrine, Edwards was careful, amid all his Pietism, to keep intact the older view of Puritan social responsibility in what was, above all, a matter for him of faith, belief, and trust in God.

4.
Philip
Schaff

The second person in our story coming from the Evangelical and Reformed tradition is Philip Schaff (1819–93). He might be considered a Unionist just as much as a Pietist because he was baptized into the Swiss Reformed Church, ordained by the German Evangelical Church of the Union in Prussia, served as a professor in the new seminary of an American church of German Reformed background, and ended his career as a noted scholar and a Presbyterian in New York City.[112] The unusual theological characteristic of Schaff was that he joined his colleague in the German Reformed seminary, John W. Nevin, in leading the "Mercersburg Theology," a churchly sacramental reaction against Puritan Revivalism (somewhat resembling the Oxford Movement in England), which might indicate anti-Pietistic tendencies coming from Schaff and Nevin.[113] But contrary to what might seem evident, Schaff always remained very much a Pietist, defining it in an irenic, inner-churchly form characteristic also of much of the later UCC.

Son of a carpenter, who died when he was a child, Philip Schaff left Switzerland at age fifteen, traveling alone to a Pietistic boys' school at Kornthal, near Stuttgart, Germany, where he received confirmation into the German Lutheran Church. There Schaff also had a Pietistic conversion experience at age seventeen, which he described thirty-five years later as follows:

> At first [this youth from Switzerland] felt lonely and discontented, and was seized by . . . homesickness. . . . One

71

day, at three o'clock in the morning, this stranger went away to the neighboring forest, and prayed, crying in intense agony, and as if on the brink of despair. His heart was without rest, because it had not yet found its rest in God. But God had mercy upon him, and heard his cry. His homesickness was the pain of a new birth from above. He began to realize for the first time what it is to have peace with God through the atoning blood of Christ. . . . By the faithful instruction and pious example of Kullen [headmaster] and Kapff [pastor], he was introduced into the mysteries of evangelical truth and dedicated himself . . . to the service of God.[114]

After finishing gymnasium studies at Stuttgart, Schaff went on to complete theological training at the leading German universities of his day. Under the massive liberal theological influence of Schleiermacher and the Pietistic church history methods of Augustus Neander, Schaff also felt the impact of Hegelianizing church history and biblical study at Tübingen, the evangelical influence of Tholuck at Halle, and the strict orthodoxy of Hengstenberg at Berlin.

Already a gifted and promising theological instructor *(Privatdozent)* at Berlin University, the twenty-four-year-old Schaff accepted a call to become professor at the struggling seminary of the German Reformed Church in Mercersburg, Pennsylvania. Ordained into the ministry of the Evangelical Prussian Union Church (the counterpart of the Evangelical Synod of the Evangelical and Reformed Church) before leaving for America, Schaff also visited in England on his way, with the following observation: "The [German] rules the world by thought; the [English] rules it by politics. . . . They complement one another. Idealism without the solid basis of realism turns to airy spiritualism; realism without idealism to bald materialism."[115]

Enjoying the strange new country, Schaff was astonished when the American church tried (and exonerated) him for heresy after his 1844 inaugural address at Mercersburg. His hearers suspected betrayal when his *Principle of Protestantism* viewed church history as a divine development leading to a merger of Protestant and Roman traditions into a renewed evangelical Catholicism.[116] Schaff thought that in America distorted subjectivism and individualism produced a sectarian spirit too negative toward sacraments, as well as an unchurchly spirit wishing to convert individual souls rather than nurturing proper communal life, and an unhistorical spirit paying insufficient attention to tradition. Thirty years of theological warfare followed as a result of the teachings of Schaff and Nevin. There were some conversions to Roman Catholicism, and the "Old Reformed" group began Ursinus College, seeking to maintain an anti-liturgical tradition. Through it all, Schaff maintained an irenic, evangelical, ecumenical spirit. The theology of Mercersburg appears to us today to be more acceptable than the sectarian, Revivalist spirit of the nineteenth century.[117]

Schaff left Mercersburg during the Civil War in 1863, becoming professor at Union Theological Seminary in New York from 1870 until his death. Although the Mercersburg Theology as such was limited in influence, Schaff became an ever more successful and productive theological scholar. Perry Miller has pointed out how ably Schaff described to Europeans the American genius for combining conservative and liberal religious traditions in a forward-looking way (in his *America,* 1854).[118] Thus, he looked toward the future, rather than backward, as some historians do. It was characteristic of Schaff that his last words were a speech on Christian unity before an unusual ecumenical body, the World Parliament of Religions at the 1893 Chicago Columbian Exposition.[119] His address closed with a description of the merits of various denominations, including the Congregationalists, whose doctrine of the church he had sharply criticized in his earlier career. "The historian," he said, "finds in every age and in every church the footprints of Christ, the abundant manifestations of his spirit, and a slow but sure progress toward that ideal church which St. Paul describes as 'the fulness of him who filleth all in all.'" Schaff had learned well how to be an American. For all his academic research and publication, unequaled by any other American church historian, Philip Schaff always had a practical focus, the upbuilding of the church's present and future life. That interest is thoroughly in accord with the characteristics of the UCC.

5.
Andreas
Irion

The third Evangelical and Reformed person considered here was another German immigrant theological professor and representative of Pietism at the Missouri seminary of the Evangelical Synod in the Midwest. Andreas Irion (1823–70) had a less distinguished educational background and influence than Philip Schaff, but he was even more clearly a Pietist, interested in education, catechetics, and the irenic nurture of Christian communities.[120] Lacking university education, the Swabian Irion was a remarkably intellectual Pietist, having enjoyed only six years of theological training at the Basel Mission Institute. Irion's sponsorship by a mission institute was significant, as was his immigration to the then Western American frontier, where the English language took two generations longer to become predominant in German-American culture and church life.

Evangelical immigrants to the Midwest were familiar with the 1817 United Evangelical Church of Prussia, proclaimed by King Frederick William III of Prussia. His union of former Lutheran and Reformed churches had become possible because Enlightenment criticism had undermined confessional particularity, and Pietist inwardness sought spiritual truth rather than doctrinal forms of religion. "Evangelical" came to have a new, "union" meaning. Between 1830 and 1845, 40,000 new German immigrants settled in Missouri and Illinois. In 1840 at St. Louis, six pastors founded the Evangelical Church Association of the West (*Evangelischer Kirchenverein des Westens*), the organizing center for German Protestant Unionism, which became part of the Evangelical and Reformed Church in 1934.[121]

One hundred fifty-eight pastors of what came to be known as the Evangelical Synod of North America arrived in the United States as missionaries of the Basel Mission, beginning with Friedrich Schmid in Michigan (1833) and continuing until 1937.[122] By 1850 an Evangelical Seminary, the predecessor of the present Eden Theological Seminary, had begun at Marthasville, Missouri. It was fitting that Basel should provide an early teacher and second president of the Evangelical Seminary with its own Andreas Irion, where he served from 1853 until his death in 1870. After he had completed his mission training at Basel, Irion was commissioned to serve a German church near Tiflis, Russia, because his health was too poor for tropical service. He never went to Russia because the government barred any additional Swiss people from entering the country. For a short time thereafter, Irion did mission work among the Jews of Strassburg, where he also met his future, German-speaking, wife.

The mission committee in Basel finally assigned Irion to serve in North America, suggesting that he devote himself to teaching if possible. The Missouri Evangelicals had appealed to Basel for a second professor at their new seminary. After Irion and Wilhelmine Keck were married in New York, the couple set out for the three-week journey to the German seminary in the remote wilderness. Irion's inaugural address at Marthasville in June 1853 is in interesting contrast to Schaff's at Reading nine years earlier. For his texts Irion used the daily Moravian devotional passages from Daniel 2:21 ("[God] changes times and seasons . . . he gives wisdom to the wise and knowledge to those who have understanding") and Romans 12:12 ("Rejoice in your hope, be patient in tribulation, be constant in prayer"). The *Kirchenverein*, he said, was to be mindful that true wisdom comes from God alone. Human hopes pinned on Irion might be all right, if the members had first grounded their hopes in God. The New Testament word spoke peculiarly to his new seminary family. The seclusion from the world did not greatly endanger the institution from without. But the preservation of the spirit within depended on the apostle Paul's words, "Be kindly affectioned one toward another in brotherly love." What else was there to say? *"In des Herrn Willen senke ich mich hinein,"* Irion concluded, *"er mache alles wohl."*[123] Unlike his successor, Prof. Karl Emil Otto, Irion was not troubled by charges of theological heresy.

Yet the Pietistic Irion had a profound intellectual influence on his students and the Evangelical Synod through the seventeen remaining years of his life, especially after 1857, when he became seminary president. A later professor, F. Mayer, summarized Irion's life as follows.

> Andreas Irion was a deep thinker and a pious, learned divine. He absorbed the German theology of his day, especially that of his Basel teacher, Gess. Then through his individual thinking, using constructive personal methods, Irion sharpened the insights of his seminary students into the divine depths of Scripture. Irion was equally effective in deepening the preaching efforts of pastors, in structuring the order of divine service for the whole Evangelical Church, and above all, in developing catechetical instruction for the young, all of which influenced greatly the religious life of the whole church.[124]

When a second seminary building was needed at Marthasville, Irion, with his working-class background, directed and aided the students in quarrying stone, hauling it to the site, and building a two-story "upper lecture hall," which still stands. Thus, Irion's $300-a-year salary was a good investment for the Evangelical Synod! He edited without remuneration the church periodical *Der Friedensbote* ("Messenger of Peace") from 1857 to 1867 at a profit for the church. He also helped to prepare the German *Agende* (Book of Worship), which set the standard for the moderately liturgical worship of the Evangelical Synod. The St. Louis Evangelicals had also published their own *Evangelical Catechism* in 1847, based on Luther's and the Heidelberg catechisms. It contained ninety-two pages and needed revision. Laboring for many years, Irion and others completed a revision of the catechism, published in German in 1862 as the *Small Evangelical Catechism*. By 1892 it had been translated and published in English, although teaching in English at the seminary was not usual until about 1906, when Samuel D. Press was appointed the first full-time English professor.[125] Thus Irion, unlike Schaff, represented a German immigrant generation in America that had not yet made the inevitable transition to the English language.

Yet the ethnic narrowness of Irion was also a strength. Despite his early death, Irion's 242-page *Explanation of the Small Evangelical Catechism,* published posthumously in 1870, presented his thoroughly evangelical perspective, occupying a clear position between the narrowly confessional and the modernizing views. Irion's teaching, described as Pietistic, strictly Lutheran, highly speculative, and very logical, but at the same time strictly orthodox, represented the authentic Pietistic character of the Evangelicals, as well as the Unionist position, to be considered in chapter 5. Taking a Lutheran view of the presence of Christ in the Lord's Supper, Irion remained true to the union standpoint, respecting the Reformed position, and never represented his private opinion, which he took no pains to conceal, as the union consensus. Kamphausen's summary was that "Irion taught our ministers to think, while at the same time making them aware that believing means living, and not holding opinions."[126]

Never physically strong, the pioneer professor died in 1870 and was laid to rest in a small wooded cemetery on a hillside. On the simple marble slab marking Andreas Irion's grave at Marthasville is the following Pietist inscription: "And those who are wise [Luther's translation: 'the teachers'] shall shine like the brightness of the firmament; and those who turn many to righteousness, like the stars for ever and ever [Dan. 12:3]."

Chapter Five
Unionist

This chapter considers a third major component of UCC religious typology—Unionism. As one surveys nineteenth-century efforts at American church unity moving into the twentieth and twenty-first centuries, the threefold typology of Lefferts A. Loetscher may be referred to.[127] The three approaches are (1) cooperation by individuals in nondenominational bodies, (2) federative action by denominational bodies, and (3) organic union, usually "on the basis of the minimal tenets of the initiating group." Congregationalists led in this development, along with the slightly different emphases of Christian leaders (so far not discussed here), and the Unionism of the Evangelical and the Reformed leading personalities.

In the early nineteenth century the characteristic form of American religious life was developed, namely, denominations, defined as voluntary associations having common purposes (not the older church types related to the state or theologically defined).[128] As one would expect, because of their more organic view of responsibility to the whole community, Congregationalists remained aloof from this rush toward denominationalism. While other denominations were developing, Congregationalists supported a group of voluntary benevolent societies of national scope but committed to the extension of undenominational evangelical Protestantism. Only after the 1830s, when voluntary benevolent societies suffered competition from denominations, did Congregationalists begin to develop their own denominational perspectives within American pluralism. Despite a Plan of Union to cooperate in founding Congregational and Presbyterian churches in frontier missions between 1801 and 1852, for its first 200 years Congregationalism had become thoroughly decentralized. A national organization was not formed until 1852, when the Albany Convention ended the Plan of Union, supported the new Church Building Society, and began the modern yearbook.

Congregationalists led in developing cooperation in nondenominational bodies. They initiated the first American foreign mission society, the American Board of Commissioners for Foreign Missions (1810)—working also with Presbyterians and Reformed—which had sent out 2,066 missionaries by 1894.[129] They pioneered in developing the ecumenical American Home Missionary Society (1826), which was assisting 810 home missionaries by 1837.[130] Their cooperative American Education Society (1815), seeking to remedy the shortage of educated ministers, by 1838 was assisting 1,141 students. A second group of nondenominational social reform societies sought to establish a Christian American nation, incarnating the Unionist ideals of Pietism and Puritan New England. These included the American Society for the Promotion of Temperance (1826), the American Peace Society (1828), and the American Anti-Slavery Society (1833). In addition to these two approaches, the World's Evangelical Alliance was formed in London in 1846 by 800 European and American religious leaders. Philip Schaff organized a powerful American Branch of this movement in 1867; it never was able to move, however, beyond functioning as an alliance of individuals.

As seen, Philip Schaff made a leading proposal of the second type in the nineteenth century, seeking federative action by denominational bodies. Just before his death, in 1893, Schaff pleaded in Chicago before the Evangelical Alliance for "the Reunion of Christendom," a dramatic appeal for federal union.[131] "Federal union," he said, "is a voluntary association of different churches, . . . each retaining its freedom and independence in the management of its internal affairs, but all recognizing one another as sisters with equal rights, and cooperating in general enterprises, such as the spread of the Gospel at home and abroad."[132]

Although nineteenth-century proposals for the third ecumenical type, organic union, were made by the Lutheran Samuel Schmucker, the Episcopalian William Reed Huntington, the Christian Barton W. Stone, and the German Reformed Nevin and Schaff, the closest approach to organic union of separate theological traditions actually achieved was the Evangelical Synod, uniting

Lutheran and Reformed traditions on the western frontier after 1840 (although even standard historical accounts often overlook this fact).[133] Besides the union of the Disciples with many of the Christians in 1832 (which will be referred to again in connection with Barton W. Stone), the regional Plan of Union between Congregationalists and Presbyterians came close to organic union between 1801 and 1852.[134] Historians differ in explaining the failure of that union. The divisive frontier spirit figured prominently, as did reviving denominationalism. Douglas Horton has argued that two doctrines of the church were involved, especially since colonial Congregationalists amid change had not yet acquired their present view of the church.[135] Moreover, Presbyterians tolerated slavery, whereas Congregationalists tried to abolish it. At any rate, Congregationalist, Christian, Evangelical, and Reformed people and leaders have become as much or more interested in church union, especially in practice, as any other American Christians.

1.
Barton W.
Stone

Of the four main branches within the UCC, the Christians are distinctive, with their indigenous American frontier origin, although their best-known leader, Alexander Campbell, was an immigrant Scotsman. Campbell's Disciples, several thousand come-outers from Presbyterian and Baptist churches, united at Lexington, Kentucky, in 1832 with most of similarly originated Stone Christians, into a fellowship that has never been able to decide whether its name is "Disciples" or "Christians." The Christian Convention, which joined with the Congregationalists in 1931, was made up of the Stone Christians who did not join the Disciples, along with similar "Christian" dissenters who had originated among Virginia Methodists and Vermont Baptists. The oddity of the whole Christian tradition is its heartfelt desire to unite the whole body of Christ, while its down-to-earth characteristic appears to have been separation from existing ecclesiastical bodies. Thus the Separatist tradition of the Protestant Reformation, partially represented within Congregationalism, appears in a complex ecumenical form among nineteenth-century American Christians.

The first of the three groups calling themselves Christian (later Congregational Christian) was founded in 1794 by James O'Kelly, a Revolutionary War veteran and Methodist lay preacher from Virginia, who opposed bishops and left Methodism with about 1,000 dissenters. Known first as Republican Methodists, O'Kelly, Rice Haggard, and their followers in the South adopted as their new name "The Christian Church" and declared that the Bible should be their only guide. The second group calling itself Christian was based in New England. Members were followers of Elias and Abner Jones, both of whom had withdrawn from the Baptists. This group gradually became a rural Revivalist movement with Unitarian tendencies. Elias Smith, the more volatile leader, began a pioneer religious journal, the *Herald of Gospel Liberty*, in 1808. In 1845 a sectional New England Christian Convention was begun, followed in 1856 by organization of the Southern Christian Convention by North Carolina Christians.

The third Christian group was begun by Barton W. Stone (1772–1852), who was born in Maryland just before the American Revolution.[136] His widowed mother moved the family to backwoods Virginia, where young Stone developed a passion for religious freedom, skepticism of church structures, and preference for the Bible over theology and creeds. At an academy in North Carolina, Stone worried more about his soul than about his studies. Finally, in 1791, Stone came to believe that God is love and that he need no longer be fearful. A licensed Presbyterian minister, Stone taught and preached in Georgia, South Carolina, and Tennessee before receiving local ordination as pastor at Cane Ridge, Kentucky.

In 1801 Barton Stone, as the minister in charge, was responsible for the great Cane Ridge camp meeting revival, planned as a "sacramental meeting" for Presbyterians, Methodists, and Baptists. The revival impressed him not only with its unprecedented emotional power, but also with the conviction that if ministers of different faiths could preach together and save souls, the movement could continue until the whole church of Christ on earth had become one. Presbyterian opposition to the revival forced Stone and four friends to withdraw in 1803, setting up an independent Springfield (Kentucky) Presbytery. It was dissolved, however, in 1804, as Stone said, "to sink into the general body of Christian, taking no other name than Christian."[137] Thus Stone was advocating "fire union," the union of fire or the Spirit, as he called it, rather than external types of union, which he called "book union" (creeds), "head union" (consensus), or "water union" (immersion baptism).[138] In the 1840s Stone proposed a national conference on Christian unity based on a vague doctrinal program, and he indicated that, unlike most other Protestants, he opposed anti-Catholic movements from an ecumenical perspective.

Already in 1824, the fifty-two-year-old Stone, leader of several thousand Christians in several hundred churches, received a distinguished younger visitor in Georgetown, Kentucky—the thirty-six-year-old Alexander Campbell, able at that time to boast of only

400 Disciple followers in four churches.[139] Wary respect for each other's similar positions at that meeting led to the more famous Lexington, Kentucky meeting of 1832, which is regarded as the origin of the Disciples or the Christian Church more generally. "Union across the board" at Lexington, interestingly, did not include Alexander Campbell personally, since that Scottish stickler for process and order was holding out for the name "Disciples." Union occurred; the proper name never was agreed on. In effect, Stone turned over leadership of the movement to the younger and more dynamic Campbell. Yet the spirit of encircling love and ecumenical pursuit was found especially in Stone. The Christians who did not follow Stone into that union remained part of the Christian Connection, which eventually united with Congregationalism. Stone called the 1832 union "the very noblest act of my life."

Disciples historians still debate the relative importance of Stone and Campbell in originating their movement. For some, Stone as a "Christian" was first in time, in the ideal of unity, and in repudiating the Calvinistic system.[140] For others, Stone lacked Campbell's comprehensive doctrinal vigor and personal force, failing to bring the eastern Christians and not all the western Christians into the 1832 union.[141] All seem to agree that Stone's contribution "was his ecumenical charisma, his unadulterated passion for the unity of God's people, and his personal witness that visible unity is the essential calling of the Church."[142]

I have spoken more broadly about the Disciples-Christian movement because serious conversations to consider possible further union have been carried on since the 1970s between the Christian Church (Disciples of Christ) and the UCC.[143] The smaller group of Christians today within the UCC, located mainly in Ohio, Indiana, and North Carolina, had grown to about 100,000 members by the time of union in 1931.[144] Like the larger group of Disciples, they have made distinguished contributions in religious journalism and education and have strengthened the place of women and blacks in the church. Among other educational institutions begun by the Christians are Defiance College, in Defiance, Ohio (1850), and Elon College, in Elon College, North Carolina (1889). The democratic social structure of the Christian Church allowed the Virginia Christian Conference to recognize an Ohio minister's wife, the former Rebecca L. Chaney, as her husband's official associate in preaching in 1839. The Christian Church became the first denomination to recognize the ordination of a woman, Melissa Terrel, ordained to Christian ministry in 1867 at Ebenezer Church in Clark County, Ohio. (Antoinette Brown's ordination to the Congregational ministry at Butler, New York, in 1853 was recognized only by her local church.)

James O'Kelly's denunciation of slavery in 1789 had attracted many blacks to join Christian churches in the South, as did later revivals and zeal for humanitarian reform. Separate black churches were not organized before the Civil War, and in 1852, Isaac Scott, a black from North Carolina, was ordained by the Christian Church and sent to Liberia as the first overseas missionary from that denomination. After the Civil War, black Christian churches grew to include 30,000 members in 165 congregations (by 1929). In a recent assessment of the Congregational-Christian union after fifty years, Richard H. Taylor has pointed out that the union has been successful in the South among both whites and blacks.[145] Recently, the Rev. J. Taylor Stanley (among others), himself a black Congregationalist, worked at reversing dominance in the UCC by middle-class black Congregationalists over rural black Christians, who made up more than two thirds of the black UCC constituency in the South.[146] The failure of the Congregational-Christian union from the Christian perspective was that three fourths of the white Christian churches in rural areas with poorly educated ministers have been lost to the United Church, while the few urban, middle-class Christian churches have been absorbed into Congregationalism. Taylor noted that at the time of the Congregational-Christian merger, only 76 of 450 active Christian ministers had both college and seminary training. Thus, even in the UCC, the old problem of clerical aristocracy, against which Stone fought, continues to interfere with the pluralistic inclusivity to which the church is officially dedicated.

2.
Horace
Bushnell

For the other nineteenth-century representative of Congregationalism besides Harriet Beecher Stowe, I have selected the "father of American religious liberalism," Horace Bushnell (1802–76).[147] A major figure in U.S. intellectual history, Bushnell mediated between old Puritan orthodoxy and the new romantic impulses, as he sought to deliver theological orthodoxy, first, from a Revivalism "that ignored the law of Christian growth"; second, from a conception of the Trinity bordering on tritheism; third, from a view of miracles that implied a suspension of natural law; and fourth, from a theory of the atonement that "failed to declare the law of human life."[148] Seemingly a political conservative, interpreting the Civil War in terms of collective guilt, Bushnell at the same time influenced greatly the development of later liberalism and the Social Gospel. His emphasis on human growth and the symbolic use of religious language, his concern for environment and family life, his condemnation of irresponsible individualism, and his insights into moral experience made Bushnell an important part of the Unionist tradition and of the characteristic recent stance of the UCC.

Born in rural Connecticut of a Methodist farmer father and an Episcopal mother, Horace Bushnell slowly found his way to becoming a great Congregational preacher. After receiving his baccalaureate from Yale (1827), he tried teaching, commerce, and law, until something of a conversion experience led him to the liberal revivalist Yale Divinity School of Nathaniel W. Taylor. Later Bushnell confessed that reading Coleridge's *Aids to Reflection* and Schleiermacher on the Trinity helped him to find a new view of Christianity. Ordained in 1833, Bushnell became pastor at North Congregational Church in Hartford, where he served until his retirement, stimulated by an urban, socially aspiring, controversy-torn local church. There he learned to mediate between old Congregational theology and church understanding and yet to awaken those "who believed in reform, self-improvement, and gentility, who were nervous and nostalgic about the faith of their fathers, who were affronted by Calvinistic accusations and bored by theology."[149] His first and most famous book, *Christian Nurture* (1847), was a critique of the prevailing emphasis placed on conversion experience by revivalists, stressing the church-like quality and redemptive role of the family, as well as the familial quality of the church, insisting that children of Christian parents could and should be raised in such a way that they would never know a time when they had not been Christians. Bushnell thus synthesized culture and personality, anticipating Durkheim's view that society creates moral values and Freud's view that parents implant them in their children.[150]

In similar ways, Bushnell's *God in Christ* (1849), published the same year when a mystical experience illuminated the gospel for him, issued a challenge to traditional substitutionary views of the atonement, emphasizing the social, symbolic, and evocative nature of religious language. Likewise, his *Nature and the Supernatural* (1858) sought to restore to theology and religion their poetic sensitivity to the physical world.[151] He held that nature is suffused with supernature, the free principles of will and spirit. Thus Bushnell rejected much of the literalism and legalism of his background, correlating instead natural symbols and religious imagination. He remained a moralist, interpreting God according to the principle of suffering love, seeing nature as a challenge to the human will, and being bound by the limited perspective of his own age in regard to blacks and women.

The unity and coherence of Bushnell's thought and life contributed to his expanding influence, greater perhaps than that of any other liberal theologian in American history. Suffering from ill health, Bushnell traveled widely, including California, where he selected the site for the future University of California, turning down an invitation to become its first president. After preaching an installation sermon at the First Congregational Church in San Francisco, Bushnell published his "Sermon for California" (1856), noting that California's problems were opportunities:

See what a work—a Sabbath to sanctify, churches to build, and churches and ministers of Christ to assist, learning to organize, a morality to create . . . violence to subdue, industry to enoble and fortify, . . . and prayers to lay up in the golden vials here to distill when you are gone! If your heart is with Christ, can you want anything better than this?[152]

Before 1859, when Bushnell had to resign his pastorate because of his failing health, North Church withdrew from the Hartford North Consociation (1852) to preclude a heresy trial from Bushnell's bitter opponents. Despite such opposition, and the momentary setback to church union, Bushnell's ability to assemble and present coherent arguments guaranteed his impact and the influence of his interpretation of Christianity. In a more liberal vein, Bushnell's impact and practicality was greater than that of his magnificent predecessor, Jonathan Edwards. Even more effectively than in the case of Edwards, Bushnell's moralism struck his contemporaries as being in effective balance with his esthetic gifts. One of his favorite statements could be applied to Bushnell's own life: "Power moves in the direction of hope."[153] Truly, Bushnell modeled the socially responsible faith of nineteenth-century Congregationalism.

3.
Samuel D.
Press

I turn now at last to twentieth-century representatives of the UCC, who participated directly in the difficult process of bringing that 1957 church into being. The first person to be considered, Samuel D. Press (1875–1967), was a notable product of and enthusiast for church union, growing out of a pioneer transconfessional union church, the Evangelical Synod of North America.[154] Press not only led the Evangelical and Reformed churches into unity in 1934, but also was the first to propose the UCC union in 1938, when he sent a telegram to Truman Douglass and George Gibson at a Beloit, Wisconsin, meeting of the Congregational Christian General Council, saying, "What about a rapprochement between our communions looking toward union?"[155] Also a professor and president of Eden Seminary in St. Louis, like the earlier Andreas Irion, Press benefited from the worldwide ecumenical movement of the twentieth century and joyfully led a foreign-language immigrant church into union with compatible traditions more thoroughly at home in America.

Samuel David Press was born in Wisconsin into an evangelical clerical family. His father, Gottlob, a Swabian Evangelical Pietist, had immigrated to the United States in 1866. His mother was the daughter of a Baden German Evangelical pastor, and eventually all four of Samuel's sons became American Evangelical ministers. Trained for ministry at institutions of his synod, Press especially appreciated the critical biblical and evangelical views of Karl Emil Otto and the learned theology of William Becker, his teachers at

Elmhurst College and Eden Seminary. Unable for financial reasons to take advantage of a seminary scholarship to Berlin, Samuel became a young pastor in frontier German-speaking Texas. Like several of his predecessors in this story, the twenty-four-year-old, newly married pastor in Texas experienced personal conversion in his frontier parsonage, where, he said, "my eternal anchorage in God was attested to me by God in a vision of His forgiveness by grace, pure grace."[156] A treasure of $200 finally enabled Press to study at Berlin in 1902, with Harnack, Seeberg, Wobbermin, and Delitzsch. When he later became a teacher himself at Eden Seminary, Press encouraged the best of his students to earn higher degrees, the most notable of whom were Reinhold and H. Richard Niebuhr.

After returning to Evangelical pastorates in Texas, Press, in 1908, was called as the first Eden Seminary professor to teach in the English language, becoming president from 1919 until 1941. After his retirement from Eden, Press continued to teach systematic theology for ten additional years. During the Press years at Eden, the seminary was relocated, the transition was completed to American ways, and the Evangelical Synod was about to enter the second of its two recent mergers. In accord with Evangelical traditions, Press's gentle spirit manifested three characteristics: ecumenical zeal, intellectual rigor, and social passion.[157] Representing his synod, Press was stimulated by the Faith and Order and Life and Work meetings in Stockholm (1925), Lausanne (1927), and Oxford and Edinburgh (1937). The 1937 meetings especially increased his concern for social questions, led him to call the church to deal with evil in the world, and strengthened his commitment to the forthcoming UCC merger. Press had been asked as early as 1921 by the president of the Evangelical Synod, John Baltzer, to represent the cause of union at General Conference. H. Richard Niebuhr, Press's student, had become chairperson of the Evangelical Synod committee studying church union in 1928, with Press as confidant. In the thirties Press headed the Evangelical and Reformed commission on church relations. He had first talked with Lutherans, who insisted that union should be based solely on the Augsburg Confession. "Meanwhile," Press said, "I had been impressed with the freedom from regimentation and doctrinal narrowness of both English and American Congregationalists. . . . [They] have consistently safeguarded true freedom."[158] At the same time Press did not want to let freedom degenerate into anarchy. "I have therefore never believed in local autonomy as such, for authority is not really vested in the local church. The only authority is in Jesus Christ."

Meanwhile, in 1937 a biblical colloquium began meeting in St. Louis with Press; Truman B. Douglass, pastor of Pilgrim Congregational Church; George Gibson, pastor of First Congregational Church, Webster Groves; and others, including Baptists, Methodists, Disciples, and an Anglo-Catholic Episcopalian. Out of that experience in practical ecumenicity came the inspiration or the courage for Dr. Press to send his famous telegram proposing merger between the Congregational Christian and the E & R churches. As a result of the telegram, Douglas Horton, minister and secretary of the Congregational General Council, and others met Dr. Press in Chicago. "Shortly after the meeting," Press said, "Louis W. Goebel, who had succeeded George W. Richards as President of the E & R church in 1938, suggested that the matter be handled as an overture from Douglas Horton to Dr. Richards. From that point onward conversations and meetings continued until the actual formation of the UCC in Cleveland in 1957."

Walter Brueggemann has summarized as follows Press's intellectual rigor and social passion, as well as his ecumenical zeal, which we have been sketching:

> These [three elements] were consistently rooted in an evangelical devotion to the grace of God, an open, child-like devotion which found no need and no power in more stringent doctrinal statements. He understood his work as the maintenance of that context for study, worship and nurture. He labored mightily against routinization devoid of piety, fideism devoid of intellectual rigor, churchmanship devoid of openness and social awareness. In his years, the seminary was shaped by his balance of child-like faith and passion with mature rigor and discipline.[159]

Much more than an institutionalist seeking union, Samuel Press tapped the spiritual roots of church union. He saw denominationalism as weakening the churches' "common message by their separate claims." "The true basis of spiritual unity lies in holiness," said Press. "The more the church grows spiritually, grows in grace, into Christlikeness, the more her oneness will become apparent."[160]

4.
Douglas
Horton

In marked contrast culturally to Samuel Press yet in remarkable similarity of spirit to him, Douglas Horton (1891–1968) may be described as the apologist for the UCC, using that term in its original theological meaning as providing a reasoned explanation and justification for an important action.[161] A distinguished Congregational church statesman and pioneer of ecumenicity, Douglas Horton was born in Brooklyn, graduated from Princeton, received his B.D. from Hartford Theological Seminary and his M.A. and Doctor of Sacred Theology degrees from Harvard, and did graduate work at Edinburgh; Mansfield College; Oxford, and Tübingen, Germany.

After ordination in 1915, Horton served churches in Connecticut, Massachusetts, and Chicago, Illinois. While minister in Chicago, Horton, in 1928, introduced the new Protestant theological orthodoxy from Europe to America when he translated and published Karl Barth's *The Word of God and the Word of Man.* Always interested in ecumenism, Horton, in 1937, edited the *Basic Formula for Church Union,* one of the classic documents of the ecumenical movement.[162] From 1938 until 1955 Dr. Horton headed the Congregational Christian Churches as minister and secretary of the General Council, during much of the negotiation that brought the UCC into being. He also led in helping form the World Council of Churches (WCC) and the National Council of Churches in the U.S.A. Horton served on the WCC Central Committee and chaired its Faith and Order Commission. He was moderator of the International Congregational Council from 1949 to 1953. Hailed as having a "deep concern for the church-universal" when President Nathan Pusey appointed him dean of the Harvard Divinity School in 1955, Horton gave even more time to that concern after he retired from Harvard in 1959, attending four sessions of the Vatican Ecumenical Council, reported on in four books published by United Church Press, *Vatican Diary*, 1962, 1963, 1964, and 1965. At his death, Richard Cardinal Cushing said of Horton, "He was a learned and simple man of God, . . . who was determined that every effort . . . should be expended in searching out God's will for his church." Edwin Espy, from the National Council of Churches, said that Horton spoke forcefully for Christian unity before ecumenicity had become the vogue.

For Horton, interest in the new UCC was part of his own recovery of a doctrine of the church and a theology of the whole church associated with the coming of neoorthodoxy to America. In his 1957 introduction to a reprint of his 1928 Barth translation, Horton recalled:

> It was a generation ago that I ran across the German text, published under the title *Das Wort Gottes und die Theologie*. . . . Only those who are old enough to remember the particular kind of desiccated humanism, almost empty of otherworldly content, which prevailed in many Protestant areas in the early decades of this century, can understand the surprise, the joy, the refreshment which would have been brought by the book to the ordinary . . . reader of the religious literature of the time.[163]

Horton sought in the UCC more of the whole catholic tradition than the mere preservation of congregational tradition would allow. Perhaps he even romanticized a bit the continental backgrounds of the E & R Church:

> No longer will Congregational Christian scholars trace their lineage back through American and English thought alone. Their minds will be the meeting place for Jonathan Edwards and John Calvin, for John Owen and Ulrich Zwingli. They will recognize themselves as the heirs of two opulent lines of inheritance. . . . In the coming together in worship of Puritan simplicity and the more lavish liturgy of the Mercersburg movement there will be gain.[164]

Yet in the same article Horton also referred to the pragmatic advantages of union:

> The most obvious advantage of the union is the least important and has been the least frequently mentioned: the union will constitute an out-and-out benefit to the business life of the two communions. All the features of denominational life which depend upon what is called commercially the size of the market or the breadth of the financial base will be profited.

Here Horton was calling on a motivation that the more pious Press would probably not have stressed. Indeed, in a 1950 pamphlet entitled *Of Equability and Perseverance in Well Doing,* Horton had argued that the older form of Congregational organization, suitable to agrarian economy, was inadequate for "out-guessing and out-maneuvering" the anti-Christian forces of the time. He sought a more flexible church organization, with authority to act where action was needed.[165] The desire to arm the church for effective social action battle was indeed a typical UCC perspective. How well the strategy has succeeded is open to discussion!

Douglas Horton saw clearly that Congregationalists would have to decide again what they stood for in order to enter or oppose the forthcoming union. His 1960 introduction to Walker's *Creeds and Platforms of Congregationalism* preserved Horton's conviction that the nonseparating tradition was what Congregationalists needed in their twentieth-century church life. Earlier, Horton (together with Truman B. Douglass) had been able, in 1953, to persuade the courts to reverse a previous ruling that the Congregational Christian General Council had no power to undertake a union on behalf of individual churches. Horton's argument, later developed and published under the title *Congregationalism: A Study in Church Polity,* used seventeenth- and eighteenth-century Congregational theorists to support his view that the "council is a kind of congregation."[166] Although like a congregation, the council was distinct from the local church. It had the legal right to rule itself and could not be ruled by others. Horton's theory of the council as a church not only helped his own communion to move toward union, but also helped to convince the E & R Church that Congregationalists were really committed to organic union. After plucky efforts at union on both sides, the UCC came into being on June 25–27, 1957, at Cleveland, Ohio. The efforts of the leaders proved to be successful, and a new church came into being. By 1959 a Statement of Faith (Elmer J.F. Arndt, chairperson) was approved for the new church, and in 1961 a constitution and bylaws were adopted and put into use. Thus was born the United Church of Christ.

5.
Reinhold
Niebuhr

Less directly involved in the formation of the UCC than Press and Horton, Reinhold Niebuhr became the best-known American-born theologian in the twentieth century.[167] He fits well into the Unionist category with his 1916 exhortation urging Evangelicals to move toward union with the Reformed tradition. Reinhold Niebuhr illustrates perfectly the socially responsible believer category, which I have indicated is especially typical of UCC leaders.

Niebuhr was born a favorite son of an immigrant German Evangelical minister in 1892 at Wright City, Missouri. Like his father, Reinhold graduated from Elmhurst, in 1910, and from Eden Seminary in 1913. He then received a B.D. degree from Yale Divinity School in 1914 and an M.A. degree from Yale in 1915.

Ordained an Evangelical minister in 1915, Reinhold then served for thirteen years as activist minister of a small Detroit Evangelical church, where his exposure to American industrialism turned him into a socialist critic of capitalism. Already there, Niebuhr showed that, like America itself, compounding piety and secularism, he was becoming the most religious of secular figures and the most secular of religious ones.

Niebuhr left the pastoral ministry in 1928 to teach at Union Theological Seminary, New York, where he became a great intellectual and personal force until his retirement in 1960. With a growing worldwide reputation, by the time he died in 1971 at age seventy-eight, Niebuhr had spoken everywhere and had produced seventeen major books, all seeking to reconcile faith and politics, the ideal society and human failings.

By 1932 Niebuhr, in his *Moral Man and Immoral Society,* had abandoned, in the name of Protestantism, the liberal quest for the kingdom of God on earth, in favor of Christian Realism—a liberalism tempered by deep awareness of sin. He was original in recovering neoorthodox themes, such as original sin, at a time when a liberal optimism was rampant in many liberal churches. As Walter Brueggemann has noted, "world events in the twentieth century have given Niebuhr's thought enduring credibility. Pre-Niebuhr America was romantic about the reality of evil. We thought that if we all did good, it would somehow work out."[168]

Niebuhr placed paradox and irony in the service of neoorthodox religious beliefs and liberal politics. His Evangelical teaching as a youth made him wary of the failure of the Social Gospel to impress sinners with the reality of divine retribution. But in all his mature years he continued to insist on what he called "the transcendent impossibilities of the Christian ethic of love."

As Richard Fox puts it, Niebuhr was "the prophet-priest seeking influence and humility. The German-American Anglophile. The religious-secular preacher chastising the pious and chiding the worldly. . . . The liberal crusader against liberalism. The Jamesian relativist who embraced the God of Abraham and the revelation of Jesus."[169]

Niebuhr's political activities ranged from socialism and pacifism in the early days to an effort to rally Christian support against Hitler, post-World War II resistance to Russian expansion in the Cold War, and early opposition to the Vietnam war. After World War II Niebuhr had considerable influence with policy planners in the U.S. State Department. His sense of public responsibility made him a most unusual twentieth-century clergyman.

David Brion Davis has pointed out a modern Puritan element in Reinhold Niebuhr.[170] Davis claims that the key to Niebuhr's influence was his ability to modernize the Puritan jeremiad during the decades when a growing number of college-educated intellectuals were acquiring new power in government, the press, the universities, and religious establishments.

Davis made use of Sacvan Bercovitch's definition of the American jeremiad as "a mode of public exhortation . . . designed to join social criticism to spiritual renewal."[171] No Puritan minister surpassed Niebuhr in devising a comprehensive taxonomy of sin. He was still meeting the ideological needs (as were the Puritans) of a people commissioned by God amidst sin to build a new Jerusalem in the wilderness. Thus he, too, was seeking to tame, chasten, and purify the American liberal tradition.

If Niebuhr can be included easily within the Puritan tradition, he was no less a Pietist, deriving from his heritage and tradition. His biblical, personal, dramatic, and historical categories were derived from the Pietistic family, church, and educational institutions in which he grew up.

Niebuhr failed to give sufficient credit to positive Pietistic elements in his own Evangelical upbringing. In the *Nature and Destiny of Man* he referred to Pietism as "a perfectionistic impulse in sectarian Christianity" or an "impulse toward the fulfillment of history in sectarian radicalism," quite unlike the conservative Lutheran and Reformed traditions with which he identified.[172]

Although the distinction he made is apt, Niebuhr's own background might more accurately be described as combining Pietistic inwardness with Protestant theologizing. Thus, he embodied in his own background and experience the Puritan, Pietist, Unionist, and socially responsible motifs that I have selected as characteristic of the UCC.

In regard to the denominational issue of Unionism, Niebuhr published an article entitled "Where Shall We Go?" in the March 1919 issue of the Evangelical theological magazine.[173] Stimulated by his attendance as a delegate at a 1918 conference on organic union called by the Presbyterian Church U.S.A., he presented a strong argument that the Missouri German churches, with their Lutheran piety, should choose to enter a union with Pennsylvania Germans of the Reformed faith.

In an already Unionist tradition, Niebuhr argued that "the step toward adoption of an adequate policy for the modern situation is the acquisition of a finer Christian modesty and a greater readiness to accommodate ourselves to the positions of other denominations than those with which our tradition is connected." He noted that some say Calvinism is moralistic, making salvation too much a matter of our own enterprise.

> Calvin was ambitious to influence political life in Geneva and Knox was a prophet in Scotland while Luther religiously refrained, . . . from exerting influence upon social-political problems in Germany. Calvinism has been moralistic in the best sense of the word. If there has been an overemphasis in American church life upon the need of

personal effort in finding salvation that has been Methodistic and not Calvinistic.[174]

Thus, in both the realms of public responsibility and churchly Unionism, Reinhold Niebuhr argued persuasively that just as America should forsake its chauvinistic pride and isolationism in favor of worldwide responsibilities, so also the denominations should overcome provincial loyalties in favor of moving toward true Christian unity. As a good Evangelical, and a full citizen of the modern world, Reinhold Niebuhr effectively demonstrated that his ecumenical and international insights sprang logically and constructively from a deep understanding and appreciation of his own denomination and loyalty to his own country.

6.
Robert V.
Moss

My final representative of twentieth-century UCC leaders com-
mited to Unionism is the second president of the UCC, Robert V.
Moss (1922–76).[175] Born within a church-related family of the
North Carolina Reformed Church, Moss graduated from Franklin
and Marshall College, Lancaster, Pennsylvania, and from Lancaster Theological Seminary, teaching religion at the former institution from 1946 to 1950. Ordained into the E & R Church in
1946, Robert Moss received a Ph.D. degree in New Testament from
the University of Chicago Divinity School in 1954, having already
become a professor of New Testament at Lancaster Seminary in
1950. In 1957, at age thirty-five, he was appointed seminary president but also continued teaching.

Elected president of the UCC in 1969, Moss gave distinguished
service for just under eight years, in a troubled time for both
church and society, before dying of cancer at age fifty-four. J.
Martin Bailey recalls that

> when [Moss] was elected in 1969, the United Church of
> Christ was uncertain about the roles that youth, blacks, and
> the articulate advocates of various causes should play. Bob
> knew how to encourage responsible participation. His in-
> stallation in February 1970 was a joyous celebration of trust
> and unity. He grasped, more quickly than most, the signifi-
> cance for the church of the emerging women's movement.
> Because he believed in them, a task force of UCC women

helped liberate men as well as women from stereotypes that have limited opportunity and participation. Bob knew when to remain silent so that others could find their voices and their roles in church councils. . . . He helped the United Church respond to the '70s by pointing back to our biblical heritage and forward with confidence to the God who still works in history.[176]

A biblical scholar and theologian, Robert Moss, in accord with the temper of the UCC, led the fellowship in many areas of social concern, identified with the roots of Christianity. Although his son, John, a Vietnam veteran, was disabled from wounds suffered in the war, Dr. Moss called for amnesty for conscientious objectors. At the same time he called for greater government aid for returning veterans. He was deeply committed to racial and economic justice, to court and penal reform, and to the struggle of people everywhere for self-government and personal dignity.

Robert Moss's ecumenical enthusiasm was evident at Lancaster and became a focus for his presidency. He was a delegate observer at the Second Vatican Council. He pledged the United Church to be a uniting church. The conversations between the UCC and the Disciples were high on his agenda. Moss served on the Central Committee of the World Council of Churches and the Executive Committee of the National Council of Churches. He headed, in 1973, the first official delegation from an American church to churches in East Germany and was the first American permitted to preach in the German Democratic Republic.

During his brief final illness, Dr. Moss wrote and circulated a two-page essay on "What I Covet for the United Church of Christ Today." He made three points as he sought to encourage his life-long goal, "a growing faithfulness to the gospel of Jesus Christ." The first had to do with "the quality of our life as a Christian community," which, he said, is rooted and grounded in the local church. Second, "faithfulness to the gospel of Jesus Christ has to do with the way we care about the poor and the oppressed of the world." Third, "I think faithfulness to the gospel for the UCC today calls for it to resume its role of leadership in the movement toward church union in the U.S. today." He asked the church to reconsider how serious its members were when they said, "We are a uniting church." Moss concluded: "The passion for unity springs ultimately out of that caring for the whole human family about which I spoke . . . or as the full text of the words we chose for our emblem puts it: 'I pray that they may all be one, that the world may believe that thou hast sent me.'"[177] In Martin Bailey's words, "Bob Moss demonstrated . . . that strength and influence do not come from constitutions or political maneuvers. They spring from a generous personality and intellectual integrity. Ultimately their roots are in faithfulness to the Lord who made the heavens and the earth."[178]

Conclusion

This book has traced the lives of twenty-four persons representative of the convergence of sectarian and churchly sources providing the Puritan, Pietist, and Unionist centerpoint of UCC identity. Such persons help to suggest past models, present relevance, and future directions for socially responsible believers to function in a dangerous and promising world.

Puritans, Pietists, and Unionists in slightly different ways bore witness *in word* by vigorously preaching and teaching the ethical relevance of a covenantal-prophetic understanding of God's righteousness. They summoned moral nurture and theological guidance for those who did not yet know God, while they were able to reformulate doctrines again and again in order to meet contemporary crises.

Our socially responsible believers helped to bear special witness *in deed* as part of gathered and gathering communities able to act, guided by moral law, encouraging hopeful vision, and manifesting human compassion. Luther, Melanchthon, Zwingli, Calvin, and Ursinus initiated lasting reforms in church, school, and society. Browne, Robinson, and Ames pushed farther into congregational self-governments under God, and Cromwell partially realized the first modern political-spiritual revolution.

Cotton and Hooker relocated these traditions in colonial America, while Hutchinson and Stowe broke ground toward women/family/equality rights in a Puritan context. Mather and Edwards explored Pietist spiritual depths, while Schlatter, Schaff, and Irion showed how Reformation confessions could live on amid personal faith adaptations suitable to a non-Germanic world.

Just as these traditions today must work cooperatively with minority, Catholic, evangelical, and ecumenical communions that struggle for civil liberties, against nuclear war, against hunger, and for human rights everywhere, so Stone, Bushnell, Press, Horton, Niebuhr, and Moss helped to bring powerful Unionist traditions to bear on the possibility that a hesitating church might be reinvigorated to help redeem a present needy world.

Like other traditions, socially responsible believers within the UCC are called on today to reclaim and recast their heritages. Their treasures in earthen vessels can grow only by renewed commitment. Since Christ has come, their trust is justified that they have access to a vision so long anticipated. Believing that Christ will come again, they can live actively in an in-between time, with living memory and with sure hope. Socially responsible believers can be a sign today and tomorrow that a truly united church of Christ may yet emerge that can help to speak a saving divine word to a dying world.

Notes

1. See Martin Brecht, "Initia Christi," in *Zeitschrift für Theologie und Kirche* 74 (1977):222, and Heiko A. Oberman, *Luther: Mensch zwischen Gott und Teufel* (Berlin: Severin und Siedler, 1982), pp. 171–84.

2. See Hans-Christoph Rublack, "Luther and the Urban Social Experience," *Sixteenth Century Journal* 16 (Spring 1985):24, and Steven Ozment, *The Age of Reform, 1250–1550* (New Haven, CT: Yale University Press, 1980), pp. 260–72.

3. Peter Meinhold, *Philipp Melanchthon: Der Lehrer der Kirche* (Berlin: Lutherisches Verlagshaus, 1960), p. 136.

4. Consult John T. McNeill, *Unitive Protestantism: The Ecumenical Spirit and Its Persistent Expression* (Richmond, VA: John Knox Press, 1964).

5. A.G. Dickens, *The German Nation and Martin Luther* (New York: Harper & Row, 1974), p. 100.

6. See Bernd Moeller, *Imperial Cities and the Reformation: Three Essays* (Philadelphia: Fortress Press, 1972), and Robert C. Walton, *Zwingli's Theocracy* (Toronto: University of Toronto Press, 1967), pp. 3–16.

7. G.R. Potter, *Zwingli* (New York: Cambridge University Press, 1976). See also Jean Rilliet, *Zwingli, Third Man of the Reformation* (Philadelphia: Westminster Press, 1964).

8. For "prophesying," see Patrick Collinson, *The Elizabethan Puritan Movement* (Berkeley: University of California Press, 1967), pp. 168–76; Peter Toon, *Puritans and Calvinism* (Swengel, PA:

Reiner Publications, 1973), p. 17; and R.W. Dale, *History of English Congregationalism* (London: Hodder & Stoughton, 1907), p. 103.

9. Wilhelm H. Neuser, *Die Reformatorische Wende bei Zwingli* (Neukirchen-Vluyn: Neukirchener Verlag, 1977), p. 145. Compare also A. Rich, *Die Anfänge der Theologie Huldrych Zwingli* (Zurich, 1949).

10. See Lowell H. Zuck, ed., *Christianity and Revolution: Radical Christian Testimonies, 1520–1650* (Philadelphia: Temple University Press, 1975), for both Anabaptist and Puritan documents.

11. See Erik Wolf, *Die Sozialtheologie Zwinglis*, from *Festschrift Guido Kisch* (Stuttgart, 1955).

12. Zwingli's *Sämtliche Werke* (Zurich, 1908, 1982), 2:58–59.

13. On Bucer, see Wilhelm Pauck, ed., *Melanchthon and Bucer*, Library of Christian Classics, 19 (Philadelphia: Westminster Press, 1969); Constantine Hopf, *Martin Bucer and the English Reformation* (Oxford: Basil Blackwell, 1946); and W.P. Stephens, *The Holy Spirit in the Theology of Bucer* (New York: Cambridge University Press, 1970).

14. On Calvin, see François Wendel, *Calvin: The Origins and Development of His Religious Thought* (New York: Harper & Row, 1963), and T.H.L. Parker, *John Calvin: A Biography* (Philadelphia: Westminster Press, 1975).

15. For Reformed confessions of faith, including the Tetrapolitana, consult Arthur C. Cochrane, ed., *Reformed Confessions of the Sixteenth Century* (Philadelphia: Westminster Press, 1966).

16. For Bullinger, see J. Wayne Baker, *Bullinger and the Covenant: The Other Reformed Tradition* (Athens: Ohio University Press, 1980).

17. Wilhelm Pauck, "Calvin and Butzer," *Journal of Religion* (1929), pp. 237–56, reprinted in Pauck, *The Heritage of the Reformation* (New York: Oxford University Press, 1968), pp. 85–99; Hastings Eells, "Martin Butzer and the Conversion of John Calvin," *Princeton Theological Review* 23 (1924):402–19.

18. For Bullinger's confessions, see Cochrane, *Reformed Confessions*, pp. 220–301.

19. See "The Making of a Reforming Prince: Frederick III, Elector Palatinate" by Owen Chadwick, in R. Buick Knox, ed., *Reformation, Conformity, and Dissent* (London: Epworth Press, 1977), pp. 44–69.

20. On Ursinus, see Derk Visser, "Zacharias Ursinus," in Jill Raitt, ed., *Shapers of Religious Traditions in Germany, Switzerland, and Poland, 1560–1600* (New Haven: Yale University Press, 1981),

pp. 121–39, and Derk Visser, *Zacharias Ursinus* (New York: The Pilgrim Press, 1983).

21. For Ursinus' development, see Erdmann K. Sturm, *Der junge Ursinus. Sein Weg von Philippismus zum Calvinismus (1534–1562)* (Neukirchen-Vluyn: Neukirchener Verlag, 1972).

22. See J.F.G. Goeters, "Entstehung und frühgeschichte des Katechismus," pp. 7ff., from Lothar Coenen, ed., *Handbuch zum Heidelberger Katechismus* (Neukirchen-Vluyn: Neukirchener Verlag, 1963).

23. J. Michael Reu has shown that Ursinus derived the three-point form of the Heidelberg Catechism from a 1547 Lutheran catechism printed at Regensburg, written by a layman for home use, and reprinted in Heidelberg, 1558. (Reu, *Süddeutsche Katechismen*, vol. 1 of *Quellen zur Geschichte des Katechismus-Unterrichts* (Gütersloh: Bertelsmann, 1904), pp. 198, 444, 720.

24. See August Lang, *Der Heidelberger Katechismus und Vier Verwandte Katechismen* (Leipzig, 1907), vol. 3, and Walter Hollweg, *Neue Untersuchungen zur Geschichte und Lehre des Heidelberger Katechismus* (Neukirchen: Neukirchener Verlag, 1961).

25. Visser, "Zacharias Ursinus," p. 128.

26. See the discussion in Emile G. Leonard, *A History of Protestantism, 2. The Establishment* (Indianapolis: Bobbs-Merrill, 1968), vol. II, pp. 15–26.

27. See Gustav Adolf Benrath, "Zacharias Ursinus als Mensch, Christ, und Theologie," in *Reformierte Kirchenzeitung* 124 (June 15, 1983):154–58, and Karl Müller, "Zacharias Ursinus, ein Vater der evangelischen Christenheit," in *RKZ* (April 15, 1983):101–3.

28. Heinrich Heppe, *Geschichte des Pietismus und der Mystik in der reformierten Kirche, namentlich der Niederlande* (Leiden: Brill, 1879), and August Lang, *Puritanismus und Pietismus, Studien zu ihrer Entwicklung von M. Butzer bis zum Methodismus* (Neukirchen: Erziehungsvereins Neukirchen, 1941). See also F. Ernst Stoeffler, *The Rise of Evangelical Pietism* (Leiden: Brill, 1965), and Lowell H. Zuck, "Heinrich Heppe: A Melanchthonian Liberal in the 19th Century German Reformed Church," *Church History* 51 (December 1982):419–33.

29. For introductions to English Congregational history, see Geoffrey F. Nuttall, *Visible Saints: The Congregational Way, 1640–1660* (Oxford: Basil Blackwell, 1957), and R. Tudur Jones, *Congregationalism in England, 1662–1962* (London: Independent Press, 1962), pp. 13–32.

30. For a general introduction to English Congregational his-

tory, consult Horton Davies, *The English Free Churches* (New York: Oxford University Press, 1952), pp. 1–58.

31. For Anglican history, consult A.G. Dickens, *The English Reformation* (London: Batsford, 1964).

32. Regarding use of terms, see Basil Hall, "Puritanism: The Problem of Definition," in *Cambridge Studies in Church History,* ed. G.J. Cuming (Camden, NJ: Thomas Nelson & Sons, 1965), 2:283–96. For the distinction between Free Church-Congregational ecclesiology and Reformed-Presbyterian ecclesiology, see Geoffrey F. Nuttall, "Relations Between Presbyterians and Congregationalists in England," a Joint Supplement of the Congregational Historical Society *Transactions* and the Presbyterian Historical Society *Journal,* December 1964, pp. 1–7. Nuttall dates the beginnings of Congregational ecclesiology from the Anabaptist opponents of Zwingli in Zurich, 1525.

33. Erik Routley lists characteristics of Puritans in "Twilight of Puritanism," *Transactions of the Congregational Historical Society,* ed. John H. Taylor, 20 (October 1970):350–60.

34. Nuttall, *Visible Saints,* pp. 4–7.

35. For Hooper, see W.M.S. West, *John Hooper and the Origins of Puritanism* (Zurich, 1955).

36. For Browne, see B.R. White, *The English Separatist Tradition: From the Marian Martyrs to the Pilgrim Fathers* (New York: Oxford University Press, 1971), pp. 44–66, and Albert Peel and Leland H. Carlson, eds., *The Writings of Robert Harrison and Robert Browne* (London: Allen & Unwin, 1953).

37. For Robinson, see Walter H. Burgess, *John Robinson, Pastor of the Pilgrim Fathers* (London: Williams & Norgate, 1920); R. Ashton, ed., *The Works of John Robinson* (London: John Snow, 1851), 3 vols.; and Stephen Brachlow, "John Robinson and the Lure of Separatism in Pre-Revolutionary England," *Church History* 50 (September 1981):288–301.

38. See Edmund F. Jessup, *The Mayflower Story* (Retford, England: Whartons Ltd., 1969), p. 7, and Lowell H. Zuck, "Reviewing Congregational Origins Among Puritans and Separatists in England," *Bulletin of the Congregational Library* 29 (Winter 1978): 4–13.

39. John Robinson, *The Justification of Separation* (1610), in Ashton, 2:51–52, quoted by Brachlow, "John Robinson," p. 294.

40. For Ames, see Keith L. Sprunger, *The Learned Dr. William Ames* (Urbana: University of Illinois Press, 1972); Douglas Horton, trans., *William Ames* by M. Nethenus, H. Visscher, and K. Reuter (Cambridge, MA: Harvard Divinity School Library, 1965); and Lee W.

Gibbs, *William Ames: Technometry* (Philadelphia: University of Pennsylvania Press, 1979).

41. *The Winthrop Papers* (Boston: Massachusetts Historical Society, 1931), 2:180, quoted by Sprunger, *Learned Dr. William Ames*, pp. 91–92. Ames's 1623 and 1629 *Medulla Theologica* has been newly translated by John D. Eusden as *The Marrow of Theology* (New York: The Pilgrim Press, 1968).

42. See Horton, *William Ames* (Reuter), pp. 230–35.

43. Regarding analytical theology, see Otto Weber, "Analytische Theologie. Zum geschichtlichen Standort des Heidelberger Katechismus," in *Die Treue Gottes in der Geschichte der Kirche* (Gesammelte Aufsätze, 2) (Neukirchen: Neukirchener Verlag, 1968), pp. 131–46.

44. See article on "Aristotelismus" by Rolf Schäfer, in *TRE (Theologische Realenzyklopädie* (Berlin: de Gruyter, 1978), 3:791–95.

45. See Jürgen Moltmann, *Christoph Pezel (1539–1604) und der Calvinismus in Bremen* (Bremen: Verlag Einkehr, 1958), p. 92.

46. See K. Clair Davis, "The Reformed Church of Germany: Calvinists as an Influential Minority," in W. Stanford Reid, ed., *John Calvin: His Influence in the Western World* (Grand Rapids, MI: Zondervan, 1982), pp. 123–38.

47. On Ramism, see Walter J. Ong, S.J., *Ramus, Method, and the Decay of Dialog* (Cambridge, MA: Harvard University Press, 1958), and Jürgen Moltmann, "Zur Bedeutung des Petrus Ramus für Philosophie und Theologie in Calvinismus," *Zeitschrift für Kirchengeschichte* 68 (1957):295–318.

48. Biographies of Cromwell include Robert S. Paul, *The Lord Protector: Religion and Politics in the Life of Oliver Cromwell* (Grand Rapids, MI: Eerdmans, 1964); Christopher Hill, *God's Englishman: Oliver Cromwell and the English Revolution* (New York: Dial Press, 1970); and Antonia Fraser, *Cromwell: The Lord Protector* (New York: Alfred A. Knopf, 1973). See also Maurice Ashley, *The Greatness of Oliver Cromwell* (London: Hodder & Stoughten, 1957), and Charles H. Firth, *Oliver Cromwell and the Rule of the Puritans in England* (Oxford: Oxford University Press, 1953).

49. See Cromwell's letter from Bristol, September 14, 1645, in Zuck, *Christianity and Revolution*, pp. 232–34.

50. Darrett B. Rutman, *American Puritanism* (New York: W.W. Norton & Co., 1970), pp. 27, 17.

51. Robinson, *Justification*, p. 134.

52. For Brewster, see Ashbel Steele, *Chief of the Pilgrims: or the Life & Times of William Brewster* (Philadelphia: 1857; Ayer Co.

reprint); Dorothy Brewster, *William Brewster of the Mayflower* (New York: New York University Press, 1970); and Mary B. Sherwood, *Pilgrim: A Biography of William Brewster* (Falls Church, VA: Great Oak Press, 1982).

53. For Bradford, see Bradford Smith, *Bradford of Plymouth* (New York: J.B. Lippincott, 1951), and Perry D. Westbrook, *William Bradford* (Boston: Twayne Publishers, 1978).

54. William Bradford, *Of Plymouth Plantation,* ed. Francis Murphy (New York: Random House, 1981). Recent sketches of Pilgrim history appear in George D. Langdon Jr., *Pilgrim Colony* (New Haven: Yale University Press, 1966), and Robert M. Bartlett, *The Pilgrim Way* (New York: The Pilgrim Press, 1971).

55. Quoted in Langdon, *Pilgrim Colony,* p. 59.

56. For Winthrop, see Edmund S. Morgan, *The Puritan Dilemma: The Story of John Winthrop* (Boston: Little, Brown & Co., 1958).

57. For Cotton, see Larzer Ziff, *The Career of John Cotton* (Princeton, NJ: Princeton University Press, 1962), and *John Cotton on the Churches of New England* (Cambridge, MA: Harvard University Press, 1968), as well as Everett H. Emerson, *John Cotton* (New York: Twayne Publishers, 1965).

58. Edmund S. Morgan, *Visible Saints: The History of a Puritan Idea* (Ithaca, NY: Cornell University Press, 1963).

59. Ziff, *Career of John Cotton,* p. 259.

60. For Hutchinson, see Emery Battis, *Saints and Sectaries: Anne Hutchinson and the Antinomian Controversy* (Chapel Hill: University of North Carolina Press, 1962); David D. Hall, ed., *The Antinomian Controversy, 1636–1638* (Middletown, CT: Wesleyan University Press, 1968); and Kai T. Erikson, *Wayward Puritans: A Study in the Sociology of Deviance* (New York: John Wiley & Sons, 1966).

61. Hall, *Antinomian Controversy,* p. 268.

62. Most recently, see James W. Fowler and Robin W. Lovin, *Trajectories in Faith: Five Life Stories* (Nashville: Abingdon Press, 1980), and Selma R. Williams, *Divine Rebel: The Life of Anne Marbury Hutchinson* (New York: Holt, Rinehart & Winston, 1981).

63. Sacvan Bercovitch, *The Puritan Origins of the American Self* (New Haven, CT: Yale University Press, 1975), p. 93.

64. For Hooker, see Frank Shuffelton, *Thomas Hooker, 1586–1647* (Princeton, NJ: Princeton University Press, 1977); Sargent Bush Jr., *The Writings of Thomas Hooker* (Madison: University of Wisconsin Press, 1980); and George H. Williams et al., *Thomas Hooker: Writings in England and Holland, 1626–1633* (Cambridge, MA: Harvard University Press, 1975).

65. Williams et al., *Thomas Hooker,* pp. 4–5.

66. John Brown, *The Pilgrim Fathers of New England and Their Puritan Successors* (London: Religious Tract Society, 1895), p. 320.

67. Mary Jeanne Anderson Jones, *Congregational Commonwealth Connecticut, 1636–1662* (Middletown, CT: Wesleyan University Press, 1968), pp. 17–18.

68. Quoted in Mary Edwards Calhoun and Emma Lenore Mac-Alarney, *Readings from American Literature* (Boston: Ginn & Co., 1915), pp. 27–28, and in Nathaniel Morton, *New England's Memorial* (Boston: Congregational Board of Publication, 1855), pp. 154–55.

69. Bush, *Writings of Thomas Hooker,* pp. 312–13.

70. Battis, *Saints and Sectaries,* p. 247.

71. For Harriet Beecher Stowe, see Marie Caskey, *Chariot of Fire: Religion and the Beecher Family* (New Haven, CT: Yale University Press, 1978); Milton Rugoff, *The Beechers: An American Family in the Nineteenth Century* (New York: Harper & Row, 1981), p. 356; and Charles H. Foster, *The Rungless Ladder: Harriet Beecher Stowe and New England Puritanism* (Durham, N.C.: Duke University Press, 1954).

72. For Lyman Beecher, see Stuart C. Henry, *Unvanquished Pilgrim: A Portrait of Lyman Beecher* (Grand Rapids, MI: Eerdmans, 1973).

73. Caskey, *Chariot of Fire,* pp. 202–3.

74. Ibid., p. 207.

75. For example, Hajo Holborn, *A History of Modern Germany, 1648–1840* (New York: Alfred A. Knopf, 1964), p. 142: "The political and social conditions of Germany explain why the movement [Pietism] was so largely confined to certain social classes and never, like Puritanism or Methodism, aimed at a total reform of church and state but rather concentrated on the regeneration of the private life of the individual."

76. F. Ernest Stoeffler, *The Rise of Evangelical Pietism* (Leiden: Brill, 1965), pp. 27–29.

77. Ibid., pp. 13–23.

78. August Lang, *Puritanismus und Pietismus: Studien zu ihrer Entwicklung von M. Butzer bis zum Methodismus* (Neukirchen: Buchhandlung des Erziehungsvereins Neukirchen Kreis Moers, 1941).

79. Review by Martin Schmidt of Stoeffler's two volumes of the history of Pietism in *Pietismus und Neuzeit,* ed. M. Brecht et al. (Göttingen: Vandenhoeck & Ruprecht, 1976), pp. 145–49.

80. Johannes Wallmann, "Die Anfänge des Pietismus," in *Pietismus und Neuzeit,* ed. M. Brecht et al., Bd. IV (Göttingen: Vandenhoeck & Ruprecht, 1979), p. 53.

81. Hartmut Lehmann, "Absonderung und Gemeinschaft in frühen Pietismus," in *Pietismus und Neuzeit*, ed. M. Brecht et al., (Göttingen: Vandenhoeck & Ruprecht, 1976), p. 79.

82. For Cotton Mather, see David Levin, *Cotton Mather: The Young Life of the Lord's Remembrancer, 1663–1703* (Cambridge, MA: Harvard University Press, 1978), and Robert Middlekauff, *The Mathers: Three Generations of Puritan Intellectuals, 1596–1728* (New York: Oxford University Press, 1971), pp. 191–367.

83. For Mather as Pietist, see Lowell H. Zuck, "Cotton Mather and German Pietism," in *Historical Intelligencer* 2 (Fall 1982):11–16, and Richard F. Lovelace, *The American Pietism of Cotton Mather: Origins of American Evangelicalism* (Grand Rapids, MI: Eerdmans, 1979).

84. In John A. Garraty, ed., *Encyclopedia of American Biography* (New York: Harper & Row, 1974), p. 740.

85. Cotton Mather, *Small Offers Towards the Service of the Tabernacle in the Wilderness . . .* (Boston: R. Pierce, 1689), p. 37.

86. *Massachusetts Historical Society Collections*, 7th ser., VII–VIII (1911–1912), "Diary of Cotton Mather." See the second volume (VIII), covering 1709–24, p. 23.

87. Ernst Benz, "Pietist and Puritan Sources of Early Protestant World Missions," *Church History* 20 (1951):34.

88. Thomas J. Holmes, *Cotton Mather: A Bibliography of His Works* (Cambridge, MA: Harvard University Press, 1940), 2:754–55. See Kuno Francke, "Further Documents Concerning Cotton Mather and A.H. Francke," *Americana Germanica* 1 (1897):31–66.

89. Cotton Mather, *Nuncia Bona e Terra Longinqua . . .* (Boston: B. Green, for Samuel Gerrish, 1715), pp. 2, 5, and 13.

90. Hartmut Lehmann, "Pietism and Nationalism," *Church History* 51 (1982):42.

91. Lovelace, *American Pietism of Cotton Mather*, p. 68.

92. Quoted in Ernst Benz, "Ecumenical Relations Between Boston Puritanism and German Pietism: Mather and Francke," *Harvard Theological Review* 54 (1961):186.

93. Lovelace, *American Pietism of Cotton Mather*, pp. 283–84.

94. For Schlatter, see Henry Harbaugh, *The Life of Reverend Michael Schlatter* (Philadelphia, 1857), and Charles H. Glatfelter, *Pastors and People: German Lutheran and Reformed Churches in the Pennsylvania Field, 1717–1793* (Breinigsville, PA: Pennsylvania German Society, 1980), 1:117–19. Marthi Pritzker-Ehrlich has published a 343–page biography of Schlatter in German: *Michael Schlatter von St. Gallen* (Zürich: ADAG Administration & Druck AG, 1981).

95. Consult Dietmar Rothermund, *The Layman's Progress: Religious and Political Experience in Colonial Pennsylvania, 1740–1770* (Philadelphia: University of Pennsylvania Press, 1961), pp. 16–36.

96. See John B. Frantz, "The Awakening of Religion Among the German Settlers in the Middle Colonies," *William & Mary Quarterly* 33 (1976):274.

97. Alan Tully, "Literacy Levels and Educational Development in Rural Pennsylvania, 1729–1775," *Pennsylvania History* 39 (1972):310–11.

98. For Boehm, see William J. Hinke, ed., *Life and Letters of the Rev. John Philip Boehm* (Philadelphia: Publication and Sunday School Board of the Reformed Church in the U.S., 1916), and Glatfelter, *Pastors and People*, pp. 21–22.

99. For Güldin, see James Tanis, "Reformed Pietism in Colonial America," in F. Ernest Stoeffler, *Continental Pietism and Early American Christianity* (Grand Rapids, MI: Eerdmans, 1976), p. 60.

100. For Stähelin, see James Tanis, *Dutch Calvinistic Pietism in the Middle Colonies* (Leiden: Brill, 1967), p. 19, and Stoeffler, *Rise of Evangelical Pietism*, pp. 169–71.

101. Tanis, *Dutch Calvinistic Pietism*, p. 19.

102. A copy of this work is in the Lancaster (PA) Theological Seminary Library and in my possession.

103. Pritzger-Ehrlich, *Michael Schlatter*, p. 36. Paul Wernle, *Das reformierte Staatskirchentum und seine Ausläufer* (Tübingen, 1923), 1:136.

104. For Edwards, see Ola Elizabeth Winslow, *Jonathan Edwards, 1703–1758)* (New York: Collier Books, 1940, 1961); Perry Miller, *Jonathan Edwards* (New York: Meridian Books, 1949, 1959); and Conrad Cherry, *The Theology of Jonathan Edwards: A Reappraisal* (Garden City, NY: Doubleday Anchor Books, 1966).

105. Jonathan Edwards, *Religious Affections*, ed. John E. Smith (New Haven, CT: Yale University Press, 1959).

106. Sydney E. Ahlstrom, *A Religious History of the American People* (New Haven, CT: Yale University Press, 1972), pp. 312–13.

107. Lovelace, *American Pietism of Cotton Mather*, p. 201.

108. "Jonathan Edwards," in *The New Encyclopaedia Britannica* (Chicago: Encyclopaedia Britannica, 1974), 6:442.

109. *The Works of President Edwards*, 4 vols. (New York: 1879), 1:16–17, quoted in Ahlstrom, *A Religious History*, p. 299.

110. The issue is discussed in Conrad Cherry, *Nature and Religious Imagination: From Edwards to Bushnell* (Philadelphia: Fortress Press, 1980).

111. *Works of Edwards*, 2:261–62.

112. For Schaff, see David S. Schaff, *Philip Schaff* (New York: Charles Scribner's Sons, 1897), and James Hastings Nichols, *Romanticism in American Theology: Nevin and Schaff at Mercersburg* (Chicago: University of Chicago Press, 1961).

113. For Mercersburg theology, see James H. Nichols, ed., *The Mercersburg Theology* (New York: Oxford University Press, 1966), and James M. Maxwell, *Worship and Reformed Theology: The Liturgical Lessons of Mercersburg* (Pittsburgh: Pickwick Press, 1976).

114. Schaff, *Philip Schaff*, pp. 12–13.

115. George W. Richards, "The Life and Work of Philip Schaff," in *Bulletin, Theological Seminary of the Evangelical and Reformed Church in the United States* 15 (1944):162.

116. Philip Schaff, *The Principle of Protestantism as Related to the Present State of the Church* (Chambersburg, PA, 1845).

117. See George H. Bricker, "A Brief History of the Mercersburg Movement," *An Occasional Paper Published by Lancaster Theological Seminary* (Lancaster, PA, 1981), pp. 10–21.

118. Philip Schaff, *America: A Sketch of Its Political, Social, and Religious Character* (1854; reprint, Cambridge, MA: Harvard University Press, 1961), editor's introduction, Perry Miller, p. xxvii.

119. See John B. Payne, "Philip Schaff: Christian Scholar, Historian and Ecumenist," in *Historical Intelligencer, Historical Journal of the United Church of Christ* 2 (1982):17–24.

120. For Andreas Irion, see John W. Flucke, *Evangelical Pioneers* (St. Louis: Eden Publishing House, 1931), pp. 127–40, and Carl E. Schneider, *The German Church on the American Frontier* (St. Louis: Eden Publishing House, 1939), pp. 314–18, 416–17.

121. Besides Schneider, summaries of Evangelical and Reformed history can be found in David Dunn, ed., *A History of the Evangelical and Reformed Church* (Philadelphia: Christian Education Press, 1961), and *Festival of the Church: Celebrating the Legacy of the Evangelical Synod of North America* (St. Louis: Office for Church Life and Leadership, 1978).

122. David Georg Gelzer, "Mission to America, Being a History of the Work of the Basel Foreign Missions Society in America" (diss., Yale University, 1952). Copy in Eden Archives, St. Louis.

123. Ibid., pp. 221–22.

124. H. Kamphausen, *Geschichte des Religiösen Lebens in der Deutschen Evangelischen Synode von Nord-Amerika* (St. Louis: Eden Publishing House, 1924), p. i.

125. Carl E. Schneider, *History of the Theological Seminary of the Evangelical Church*, Jubilee Souvenir, New Eden (St. Louis: Eden Publishing House, 1925), p. 46.

126. Kamphausen, *Geschichte des Religiösen Lebens*, p. 157.

127. Lefferts A. Loetscher, "The Problem of Christian Unity in Early Nineteenth Century America," *Church History* 32 (1963):6–7.

128. Samuel C. Pearson Jr., "From Church to Denomination: American Congregationalism in the Nineteenth Century," *Church History* 38 (1969):67–87.

129. Williston Walker, *A History of the Congregational Churches in the United States* (New York: Christian Literature Co., 1894), p. 326.

130. Pearson, "From Church to Denomination," p. 70.

131. Philip Schaff, *The Reunion of Christendom* (New York: Evangelical Alliance, 1893), quoted in Paul A. Crow Jr., "Impulses Toward Christian Unity in Nineteenth Century America," *Mid-Stream* 22 (1983):427.

132. Ibid.

133. See, for example, Donald Herbert Yoder, "Christian Unity in Nineteenth-Century America," in Ruth Rouse and Stephen C. Neill, eds., *A History of the Ecumenical Movement, 1517–1948* (London: SPCK, 1954), p. 247.

134. Charles L. Zorbaugh, "The Plan of Union in Ohio," *Church History* 6 (1937):145–64, and Robert Hastings Nichols, "The Plan of Union in New York," *Church History* 5 (1936):29–51.

135. Douglas Horton, "The Plan of Union of 1801 in the United States," *The Reformed and Presbyterian World* 26 (1961):249.

136. For Barton W. Stone, see William G. West, *Barton Warren Stone: Early American Advocate of Christian Unity* (Nashville: Disciples of Christ Historical Society, 1954), and Lester G. McAllister and William E. Tucker, *Journey in Faith: A History of the Christian Church (Disciples of Christ)* (St. Louis: Bethany Press, 1975), pp. 61–88.

137. *Declaration and Address and Last Will and Testament of the Springfield Presbytery* (St. Louis: Bethany Press, 1960), quoted in Crow, "Impulses Toward Christian Unity," p. 435.

138. *Christian Messenger* 7 (1833):315.

139. Willis R. Jones, "Journey into Union: Drama and Destiny," *Discipliana* 41 (1983):9.

140. Dr. E.E. Snoddy, quoted in W.B. Blakemore, "New Levels of Historical Concern Among the Disciples of Christ," *Church History* 25 (1956):275.

141. Blakemore, "New Levels of Historical Concern," p. 275.

142. Crow, "Impulses Toward Christian Unity," p. 437.

143. For a revised working paper, "Shared Life: A New Approach to Church Union," from members of the steering committee, Christian Church (Disciples of Christ) and United Church of Christ, August 1983, see *Keeping You Posted* (UCC), December 15, 1983.

144. For Christian Connection history, see Milo T. Morrill, *A*

History of the Christian Denomination in America (Dayton, OH: Christian Publishing Association, 1912), and D.T. Stokes and W.T. Scott, *A History of the Christian Church in the South* (Elon College, NC: Elon College, 1975).

145. Richard H. Taylor, "The Congregational Christian Union at Fifty Years: An Assessment," *Bulletin of the Congregational Library* 32 (1981):4–13.

146. J. Taylor Stanley, *A History of Black Congregational Christian Churches of the South* (New York: United Church Press, 1978), pp. 49–61, 115–28.

147. For Bushnell, see Barbara M. Cross, *Horace Bushnell: Minister to a Changing America* (Chicago: University of Chicago Press, 1958), and H. Shelton Smith, ed., *Horace Bushnell* (New York: Oxford University Press, 1965).

148. Theodore T. Munger, *Horace Bushnell: Preacher and Theologian* (Boston: Houghton Mifflin & Co., 1899), p. 387.

149. Cross, *Horace Bushnell*, p. 157, quoted by Ahlstrom, *A Religious History*, p. 610.

150. See Daniel Walker Howe, "The Social Science of Horace Bushnell," *Journal of American History* 70 (1983), p. 317.

151. Conrad Cherry, *Nature and Religious Imagination: From Edwards to Bushnell* (Philadelphia: Fortress Press, 1980), p. 234.

152. Quoted in a sermon by William G. Chrystal at First Congregational United Church of Christ, Stockton, CA, February 21, 1982.

153. John Leslie Lobingier, *Pilgrims and Pioneers in the Congregational Christian Tradition* (New York: United Church Press, 1965), p. 87.

154. For Press, see David Dunn, ed., *A History of the Evangelical and Reformed Church* (Philadelphia: Christian Education Press, 1961), pp. 232, 258–59, 281, and Louis H. Gunnemann, *The Shaping of the United Church of Christ* (New York: The Pilgrim Press, 1977), p. 20.

155. Gunnemann, *Shaping*, p. 21, and "The Church Union Memoirs of Samuel D. Press," *United Church Herald* 8 (1965):21.

156. S.D. Press, "Reflections," typewritten autobiographical reflections, in Eden Archives, St. Louis.

157. Walter Brueggemann, *Ethos and Ecumenism, An Evangelical Blend* (St. Louis: Eden Publishing House, 1975), p. 7.

158. Press, "Church Union Memoirs," p. 21.

159. Brueggemann, *Ethos and Ecumenism*, p. 7.

160. William G. Chrystal, "To Hear God Speak: The Vision of Sammy Press," *A.D.*, October 1977, p. 61. See also Chrystal, "Sam-

uel D. Press: Teacher of the Niebuhrs," *Church History* 53 (1984): 504–21.

161. For Douglas Horton, see his *The United Church of Christ, Its Origins, Organization, and Role in the World Today* (New York: Thomas Nelson & Sons, 1962), introduction, and his introduction to Williston Walker, ed., *The Creeds and Platforms of Congregationalism* (Boston: Pilgrim Press, 1893, 1960), pp. vii–xvi.

162. Douglas Horton, *Basic Formula for Church Union* (Evanston, IL: Seabury-Western Theological Seminary, 1938).

163. Douglas Horton, foreword to Karl Barth, *The Word of God and the Word of Man* (New York: Harper Torchbook, 1957), pp. 1–2.

164. Douglas Horton, "Now the United Church of Christ," *Christian Century*, June 12, 1957, pp. 733–34.

165. Quoted in Gunnemann, *Shaping*, pp. 113–14.

166. See Gunnemann, *Shaping*, p. 40.

167. For Reinhold Niebuhr, see Richard Wightman Fox, *Reinhold Niebuhr, A Biography* (New York: Pantheon, 1985); June Bingham, *Courage to Change* (New York: Charles Scribner's Sons, 1961); and Charles W. Kegley, ed., *Reinhold Niebuhr: His Religious, Social, and Political Thought* (2d ed., New York: The Pilgrim Press, 1984).

168. Quoted in "Reinhold Niebuhr's Vision Persists," St. Louis *Post-Dispatch*, January 25, 1986, p. 48.

169. Fox, *Reinhold Niebuhr*, p. 291.

170. David Brion Davis, "American Jeremiah," (review of Fox's *Niebuhr*) in *New York Review of Books*, February 13, 1986, p. 7.

171. Sacvan Bercovitch, *The American Jeremiad* (Madison: University of Wisconsin Press, 1978), p. xi.

172. Niebuhr, *The Nature and Destiny of Man* (New York: Charles Scribner's Sons, 1953), 2:170, 180.

173. Reprinted in William G. Chrystal, ed., *Young Reinhold Niebuhr: His Early Writings, 1911–1931* (New York: The Pilgrim Press, 1982), pp. 101–8.

174. Ibid., pp. 106–7. "Where Shall We Go?" was first printed in the *Magazin fuer Evangelische Theologie und Kirche*, March 1919, pp. 125–30.

175. For Robert V. Moss, see Gunnemann, *Shaping*, pp. 83, 96ff.; "Robert V. Moss Is Dead at 54," *Keeping You Posted* 12 (November 15, 1976), and *History and Program: United Church of Christ* (5th ed.; New York: United Church Board for Homeland Ministries, 1986), p. 50.

176. J. Martin Bailey, "Bob Moss," *A.D.*, UCC Edition, December 1976–January 1977, p. 39.

177. Robert V. Moss, "What I Covet for the United Church of Christ Today," October 1976, mimeographed copy in Eden Archives, St. Louis.

178. J. Martin Bailey, "Presenting Our Presidents," *A.D.*, UCC Edition, December 1977–January 1978, p. K.